MW00700528

FACE-TO-FACE WITH

LOIS AND EUNICE

NURTURING FAITH *in your* FAMILY

Five Sessions for
Individuals, M&M'S (Mentors & Mentees, Friends, Family) or Groups

Includes
Leader's Guide for Facilitators

JANET THOMPSON

Martha,
leave a legacy!
Janet Thompson

NEW HOPE
PUBLISHERS
BIRMINGHAM, ALABAMA

New Hope® Publishers
P. O. Box 12065
Birmingham, AL 35202-2065
www.NewHopeDigital.com
New Hope Publishers is a division of WMU®.

Library of Congress Cataloging-in-Publication Data

Thompson, Janet, 1947-
  Face-to-face with Lois and Eunice : nurturing faith in your family : 5 sessions for individuals, M&M's (mentors & mentees, friends, family), or groups : includes leader's guide for facilitators / Janet Thompson.
    p. cm. -- (Face-to-face Bible study series)
  ISBN 978-1-59669-322-7 (sc)
 1. Families--Biblical teaching--Textbooks. 2. Interpersonal relations--Biblical teach-ing--Textbooks. 3. Families--Biblical teaching--Study and teaching. 4. Interpersonal relations--Biblical teaching--Study and teaching. I. Title.
  BS680.F3T46 2011
  227'.840071--dc23

                              2011042211

ISBN-10: 1-59669-322-3
ISBN-13: 978-1-59669-322-7

N124129 • 0112 • 2.5M1

DEDICATED WITH LOVE

To
Granny Reed

TABLE OF CONTENTS

WELCOME

My Story

I began taking steps to start the Woman to Woman Mentoring Ministry while at my home church, Saddleback Church, in Lake Forest, California, pastored by Rick Warren. "Feed My sheep" was God's call and challenge to me to go into full-time ministry. God quickly revealed that feeding was mentoring and the sheep were women in churches all over the world. In obedience to the call, I launched the ministry in my home in January 1996, and we quickly outgrew my living room. After receiving numerous requests from other churches wanting to know how to start this type of a ministry, I authored *Woman to Woman Mentoring, How to Start, Grow, and Maintain a Mentoring Ministry DVD Leader Kit* (LifeWay Press).

As I traveled throughout the United States and Canada, training and speaking on mentoring, I heard numerous requests for a Bible study depicting God's plan for mentors and mentees—"M&M'S," as we fondly call them. One morning, as my husband completed his quiet time with the Lord, Dave asked me if I had ever considered writing Bible studies based on mentoring relationships in the Bible. He knew that many M&M'S enjoy doing a Bible study together, and Dave felt that one focused on what God says about mentoring relationships would help answer many of the M&M'S questions.

After much prayer—and my husband's prodding—I decided to look in the Bible to see how many mentoring relationships I could find. Before long, I had discovered 12. This was my confirmation to begin writing the "Face-to-Face" Bible study series (formerly known as Mentoring God's Way). My passion and life mission is to help one generation of believers connect to the next generation and pass down God's plan for the Christian life. I trust that the "Face-to-Face" Bible study series will help you do exactly that.

What Is Mentoring?

I love Dee Brestin's depiction of the informality of mentoring in *The Friendships of Women Workbook:* "It's not to be a dependent relationship, but simply a friendship as you spend time with a woman who is further down the road, at least in some areas of her Christian life. Win Couchman says, 'Mentoring works very nicely over a cup of coffee.' "

For those who like more concrete and specific definitions, *Roget's Super Thesaurus* provides this explanation of the root word of mentoring. It defines *mentor* as a teacher, guide, coach, or advisor. Most dictionaries define the word *mentor* as a trusted and wise counselor. To combine

Dee's and the reference definitions with the Christian perspective: a Christian mentor is a spiritually mature woman who is a trusted and wise teacher, guide, coach, counselor, advisor, and friend. Thus, a *mentee* is someone willing to be taught, guided, coached, advised, or counseled by a trusted, wise, and spiritually older woman friend. Christian mentoring is sharing with another woman the many wonders you have seen God do in your life, and assuring her that He will do them in her life, too, as you both discover God's purpose and plan for your lives together.

Mentoring is not a hierarchy; it's always a two-way, mutually beneficial relationship where both participants learn from each other. Chris Tiegreen, author of my favorite devotional, *The One Year Walk with God Devotional,* reminds us why it is always better to seek God's ways together.

> The Bible gives us solid wisdom on which to base our lives. But while it is absolute, its interpretation can vary widely. That's where advice comes in. Never underestimate the body of Christ. He has crafted us to live in community. Wisdom usually comes not to godly individuals but to godly fellowships. Are you seeking direction? Know your heart, but do not trust it entirely. Measure it by biblical wisdom and the counsel of those who follow it well.
>
> —June 27 devotional

The Bible also clearly instructs men to mentor men and women to mentor women. Titus 2:1–8 is the traditional "mentoring" passage.

> You must teach what is in accord with sound doctrine. Teach the older men to be temperate, worthy of respect, self-controlled, and sound in faith, in love and in endurance. Likewise, teach the older women to be reverent in the way they live, not to be slanderers or addicted to much wine, but to teach what is good. Then they can train the younger women to love their husbands and children, to be self-controlled and pure, to be busy at home, to be kind, and to be subject to their husbands, so that no one will malign the word of God. Similarly, encourage the young men to be self-controlled. In everything set them an example by doing what is good. In your teaching show integrity, seriousness and soundness of speech that cannot be condemned, so that those who oppose you may be ashamed because they have nothing bad to say about us.

First Peter 5:2–4 (NLT) could be addressing mentors.

> *Care for the flock that God has entrusted to you. Watch over it willingly, not grudgingly—not for what you will get out of it, but because you are*

eager to serve God. Don't lord it over the people assigned to your care, but lead them by your own good example. And when the Great Shepherd appears, you will receive a crown of never-ending glory and honor.

A mentor doesn't need to be an expert on the Bible or God, and she doesn't need to have a perfect life. If that were the case, none of us would qualify. A mentor simply needs to be willing to share her life experiences with another woman and be an example and role model of how a Christian woman does life. And how do we learn to be a godly role model? Answer: *"Remember your leaders who taught you the word of God. Think of all the good that has come from their lives, and follow the example of their faith"* (Hebrews 13:7 NLT).

Mentoring is not doing a ministry: It is being a godly woman who follows the Lord's command: *"One generation will commend your works to another; they will tell of your mighty acts"* (Psalm 145:4).

WHO ARE M&M'S?

In the Woman to Woman Mentoring Ministry, we lovingly refer to mentors and mentees as "M&M'S"—no, that's not the candy, although we always have M&M's® candy at our events. And just like the candy, there are varieties of M&M relationships—no two are the same. M&M'S may be: friends, acquaintances, family members, workers, neighbors, members of a mentoring or other ministry, team members, women with similar life experiences, or any two women who want to grow spiritually together.

M&M'S AND MORE!

The "Face-to-Face" Bible study series has a variety of applications.
You can enjoy this study in these ways:
● On your own
● As a mentor and mentee (M&M'S) in a mentoring or discipleship relationship
● Between two friends
● Between two relatives
● As a small or large group studying together
● As a churchwide Bible study

The Bible studies offer these three types of questions:
● ON YOUR OWN—questions for doing the study individually
● M&M'S—questions for mentors and mentees, two friends, or relatives studying together
● ON YOUR OWN AND M&M'S—questions applicable to both individuals and those studying together

- Groups answer all the questions, with a Leader's/Facilitator's Guide in each book.

STUDY FORMAT

There are five main sessions, comprised of five study days. Each day's study includes:
- Scriptures and questions for you to study and answer
- Face-to-Face Reflections — a discussion of the day's topic
- Personal Parable — a story depicting and applying the day's topic
- Mentoring Moment — takeaway wisdom for the day

At the end of each session there is:
- Faith in Action — an opportunity for life application of the lessons learned
- Let's Pray Together — my prayer of agreement with you

Following session five are Closing Materials:
- Let's Pray a Closing Prayer Together
- Janet's Suggestions — ideas for further study
- Leader's Guide for Group-Study Facilitators and M&M'S
- Session Guide
- Prayer & Praise Journal

SUGGESTIONS FOR INDIVIDUAL STUDY

I admire you for seeking out this study on your own and having the desire and discipline to work on it by yourself. I like to grow in the knowledge of the Lord and His Word and have found that my most relevant insights from God come when I seek Him by myself in a quiet place. Have fun on your own, and share with someone all you are learning.

1. A good way to stay consistent in your studying is to work a little each day, during your quiet time in the morning or evening.

2. Tell someone you have started this study, and ask him or her to keep you accountable to complete it.

SUGGESTIONS FOR M&M'S— MENTORS AND MENTEES, FRIENDS, AND RELATIVES

I hope the study of *Face-to-Face with Lois and Eunice: Nurturing Faith in Your Family* adds a new dimension to your M&M relationship. Here are a few study tips:

1. Come to your meetings prepared to discuss your answers to the session's questions.

2. Or, you may decide to answer the questions together during your meetings.

3. If you don't live close, you can have phone or online discussions.

4. Remember, the questions are to enlighten and not divide; be honest and open as well as loving and kind.

SUGGESTIONS FOR GROUP STUDY

I love group studies because you get to hear other people's points of view, and lasting friendships often develop. Your meetings should be fun, informative, relevant, and applicable to group members' lives. Enjoy yourself with your fellow sisters in Christ, but remember that joining a group study does mean commitment. So please attend your scheduled meetings unless there is a real emergency. I suggest the following courtesies:

1. Put the meeting dates on your calendar.

2. Commit to doing your study and come prepared for the discussion. This honors the rest of the group, and you will get so much more from the sessions.

3. Ask questions — quite often, someone else has the same question.

4. Participate in the discussion, but be cautious of dominating the conversation. For example, if you have answered several questions, even though you know all the answers, let someone else have a turn. Try to encourage a less outgoing member to share.

5. Listen when others speak and give each speaker your full attention.

6. Arrive on time.

7. Keep in confidence the information shared in the group.

LEADERS AND FACILITATORS

When I lead and facilitate Bible-study groups, I value a complete and detailed Leader's Guide, so that is what I have provided for you. The "Face-to-Face" Bible study series has a Leader's Guide at the end of each book to provide the leader/facilitator with creative ideas for the following:

1. Guiding group discussion

2. Adding life application and variety to the sessions

3. Accommodating the varied learning styles of the group (visual learners, hands-on learners, auditory learners, and more)

TO YOU—THE READER

Whatever way you are doing this study, God has a message and a lesson just for you. Here are some suggestions I pray will enhance your experience studying *Face-to-Face with Lois and Eunice*.

1. Start each session with prayer and ask the Lord to speak to you through the Scripture readings, the prayerful answering of the questions, and the interaction with others.

2. Set your own pace. I provide breaking points, but make it comfortable for yourself and break as you need to do so.

3. If you're not sure how to answer a question, move on, but continue praying and thinking about the answer. Often my answers come quickly, but God's answers are the most fruitful.

4. Unless otherwise indicated, all the questions relate to NIV Bible passages. Lists of Scriptures are sequential, as they appear in the Bible. You will be looking up Scripture references in your Bible—an invaluable way to study and learn about the Bible.

5. Use the space provided to answer questions, but don't feel obligated to fill the space. However, if you need more room, continue answering in a separate journal.

6. A book effectively used for study should be underlined, highlighted, and comments written in the margins, so interact with this material in that way.

7. At the end of session five, you will find suggestions from me on books to read or activities, to delve deeper into what God may be teaching you about the biblical M&M relationship featured in *Lois and Eunice*.

8. Use the Prayer & Praise Journal starting on page 139 to record the mighty work God does in your life during this study. Journal prayer requests, and note when God answers.

9. Have some chocolate. After reading about M&M'S throughout the study, you'll be ready for some candy!

My heart, admiration, and encouragement go out to you with this book. I pray that mentoring becomes a vital part of your life. The "Face-to-Face" Bible study series is another way the Lord allows me to "feed My sheep." And I hope that you will enjoy this and other "Face-to-Face" Bible studies and "feed" others as well.

About His Work,
Janet

FACE-TO-FACE WITH LOIS AND EUNICE

NURTURING FAITH IN YOUR FAMILY

THEIR STORY

Can You Relate?

—Rosalie Campbell

My 20-year-old grandson, Alex, has come a long way since he reached out to me three years ago after accepting Jesus into his heart and turning away from destructive behaviors. Many mornings Alex calls, asking what God is doing in my life. I tell him about my prison ministry or issues of concern. He tells me about his struggles or joys. It's a mutual mentoring relationship: he encourages me when I need bolstering, or I encourage him with an insight from the Bible. We end our conversations by praying for each other or sharing how we're spending time with God.

When I told Alex about my early morning quiet time that includes reading from a favorite devotional, meditating on Scripture, and journaling to God, I asked if he would like a copy of the devotional and a journal. He was all for it with a bundle of questions for God. He wanted clarity about his future and what calling God had for him. It's wonderful watching my grandson mature spiritually. He inspires me with his growing faith. I'm thrilled when he says, "Nanni, I have a word from the Lord for you," or, "Do you have a word from the Lord for me?" What a joy for both of us to share those thoughts!

It's exciting to tell others what God is doing in my grandson's life and how we are prompting each other to go deeper with God.

DAY ONE

HOW DOES LOIS AND EUNICE'S
STORY RELATE TO US?

A single verse memorializes Lois and Eunice, but we can learn volumes from these two biblical representations of faithful grandmothers and mothers everywhere.

ON YOUR OWN AND M&M'S

Q: Read Acts 16:1–5 and 1 and 2 Timothy (focus on 1 Timothy 1:4–6; 2 Timothy 1:1–5; 3:10–17).

● Who was Lois? *Timothy's grandmother*

● Who was Eunice? *Timothy's mother*

● Why is it valuable to study these two women?
They raised Timothy in the faith. Taught him scripture that made him wise, complete, equipped

Q: Explain how a grandmother, mother, other family member, or member of God's family influenced your spiritual life.

My mother – church attendance, heart
girl in Milwaukee, 1st true Christian friend
Jason, teaching dates

Q: What influence do you hope to have on your grandchildren, children, or family?

Teach, encourage, inspire, equip, enjoy life tog., learn of & hear God tog. See prayers answered together.

M&M'S

Q: Discuss what you both hope to learn from this study.

FACE-TO-FACE REFLECTIONS

Before starting this study, you might not have been familiar with Lois and Eunice, but you probably recognized their grandson and son, the young pastor Timothy to whom the Apostle Paul wrote two letters in the New Testament. Paul considered Timothy his disciple, protégé, mentee, and beloved spiritual son.

Second Timothy 1:5 is the *only* place the Bible mentions the names of Lois and Eunice, but Paul including their names is significant, since often Scripture simply says "the woman" or "mother of" or "mother-in-law," or refers to grandmothers. The term *grandmother* appears one time in the Bible, and that's in reference to Lois.

Paul loved Timothy as a son and immortalized the two women responsible for the raising and spiritual nurturing of Timothy into a godly young man. We learn much about Lois and Eunice from studying the life and ministry of their grandson and son, Timothy, and his relationship with Paul, who continued the mentoring Timothy had received at home.

PERSONAL PARABLE

Like Rosalie and her grandson in the opening "Can You Relate?" story, I had a godly grandmother, Granny Reed, who spiritually poured into my life and the life of my cousins. I doubt Granny Reed thought of herself as a role model or mentor, but she provided a firm biblical foundation and an example of a woman living her beliefs. I remember Granny Reed—sitting in her favorite chair in her living room with nylons rolled down around her ankles, wire-rimmed glasses poised at the end of her nose, hair tucked into a hairnet, and her beloved Bible open in her lap—reading Bible stories to my cousins and me sitting at her feet.

Granny Reed was a "traditional" grandmother, and I'm a more contemporary "Grammie"; but just as I fondly remember Granny Reed, my prayer is that my 11 grandchildren and their parents will remember: Grammie taught us about the Bible and Jesus, and she lived what she believed.

Mentoring Moment

"All grandmas leave legacies, whether or not they have an opportunity to meet their grandchildren."
—Ellen Banks Elwell, *The Christian Grandma's Idea Book*

Day Two

Like Mother, Like Daughter

ois and Eunice's conversion to Christianity was reflected in their raising of Timothy, a cherished grandson and son. *"That precious memory triggers another: your honest faith—and what a rich faith it is, handed down from your grandmother Lois to your mother Eunice, and now to you!"*

—2 Timothy 1:5 *(The Message)*

On Your Own and M&M's

Q: Acts 14:1–23 records Paul's first trip to Lystra. What was he doing (vv. 15–17, 21–23)? *Sharing good news of Jesus. Preaching & making disciples*

● How did Lois and Eunice respond to Paul's message (2 Timothy 1:5)? *they believed with sincere faith*

Q: What was the spiritual and ethnic heritage of Eunice and of Timothy's father (Acts 16:1), and why might this deter Timothy's ministry to the Jews? *Father was a greek. Mother was a Jewish believer. Not fully a Jew*

● What did Paul do to make Timothy more acceptable to them (Acts 16:3)? *Circumcision*

Q: In Acts 15:1–32, Paul participated in the council at Jerusalem, which concluded that circumcision (Genesis 17:10–13) wasn't required for salvation. So why would Paul circumcise Timothy (1 Corinthians 10:32)?

To not offend them. Show solidarity.

Q: Write a speculative dialogue between Lois, Eunice, and Timothy's father regarding the circumcision.

L: Part of Jewish culture   F: Ridiculous - No
E: Paul said to become all things to all men
Tim: It's Timothy's decision.

Q: How has your ethnic and/or faith heritage influenced your faith?

● Did you have to renounce any family traditions or practices when you became a Christian? If so, what were they, and how difficult was it?

Q: How might your ethnicity or faith influence your children or family? *My faith should reflect Jesus & the culture of Christianity. Seeing God's goodness & love, I pray would draw my family into the kingdom.*

Q: What changes have you made that aren't biblically required, but could cause others to stumble or negatively influence your witness?

● As a Christian, what new practices did you start?

Bible reading, praying for others, ministry, worship, tithing. Involved in a church or Bible study, discipling others

M & M'S

Q: Share with each other your faith journey.

Q: Mentor, if your mentee doesn't have family support at home, assure her of your support.

Q: Mentee, what past or new practices are you struggling with as a Christian?

FACE-TO-FACE REFLECTIONS

Scholars believe that during Paul's first evangelistic missionary trip to Lystra, Lois became a Christian first, and then Eunice accepted her mother's new faith, followed by Timothy. There's no indication that Timothy's Greek father converted to Judaism or Christianity. Eunice marrying a Gentile probably means she wasn't practicing her Jewish faith at the time of their marriage, which must have saddened Lois. A Greek father, the traditional head of the family in his culture, and a non-faith-practicing mother could explain why Timothy wasn't circumcised at eight days old according to Jewish practice (Leviticus 12:3). This could hinder Timothy's credibility with the Jews who would consider Timothy a half-breed, like a Samaritan.

Even though Paul participated in the council at Jerusalem, which concluded that circumcision wasn't a requirement for salvation, Paul circumcised Timothy to expedite his acceptance in ministry. Timothy agreed to painful circumcision as a young man to remove any barriers to his witnes: he was willing to suffer for the sake of the gospel.

PERSONAL PARABLE

I spent 17 years backsliding in my faith and modeled that lifestyle to my daughter Kim, who patterned herself after my wayward example. When I repented from my sinful ways and rededicated my life to the

Lord, I thought Kim would follow me, as Eunice followed Lois. In Praying for Your Prodigal Daughter, *Kim wrote about this time in our life:*

Mom, you changed your life, and I didn't understand it and was suspicious. You expected me to change too, but I didn't want to. At the time, I liked my lifestyle, and I didn't appreciate your wanting or expecting something different for me. Today I'm glad you had a higher opinion and expectation of me than I had for myself.

Mentoring Moment

We must be willing to go beyond what is necessary
for the greater cause of advancing the gospel.

DAY THREE

SHARING YOUR TESTIMONY

*I*f you want to influence and encourage the current or next generations, you *must* let God use your story.

ON YOUR OWN AND M&M'S

Q: Read Paul's personal testimony in Acts 26:1–32 and 1 Timothy 1:12–17.

● What are the similarities and differences between the testimonies of Paul (Acts 26:4–5) and Timothy (Acts 16:1–2; 2 Timothy 3:15)?

Paul - life well-known

Jew - from childhood

Timothy - well spoke of faith via mom Greek - Christian

Q: Who did Paul focus on in his testimony (Acts 26:20–23; 1 Timothy 1:12–14; 2 Timothy 1:8)? *from childh*

Self - own story

● For what purpose did he share it (Acts 26:28–29; 1 Timothy 1:15–16)? *Bring people to Jesus*

● Why was thanksgiving and praise part of Paul's testimony?

Q: What does Paul warn about sharing our testimony
(2 Timothy 1:8)?

Do not be ashamed

Q: Write a speculative testimony that focuses on the Lord for:

- Lois   *I came to believe in Jesus in mid life when I heard the truth.*

- Eunice - *My mom shared about Jesus & I believed*

- Timothy - *"*

Q: Write your testimony. - *I grew up learning about Jesus & I believed.*

Q: Which testimony does yours most resemble: Paul's, Lois's,
Eunice's, or Timothy's? Why?   *Timothy*

Q: What does God want you to do with your testimony
(Acts 26:25–29; 2 Timothy 1:8–10)?

Share

- Like Paul in Acts 26:24 and 2 Timothy 1:11–12, what difficulties
might you encounter in sharing your testimony?
people don't understand or want to hear Think I'm crazy.

- Where will you get the courage (2 Timothy 1:12–14)?
H.S.

Q: How do Paul's testimony and Timothy's timidity
(2 Timothy 1:6–8) encourage you?

Don't be timid — go for it.

M&M'S

Q: Yesterday, you shared your story with each other. Now compose a three- to five-minute testimony focusing on the Lord, redemption, and the gospel.

● Locate a venue to share your testimony together or separately.

Q: How will your M&M relationship be a testimony?

FACE-TO-FACE REFLECTIONS

All Christians have a testimony of accepting Jesus as their personal Savior. Like Paul, some testimonies are dramatic, and others, like Timothy's, organically evolve from growing up in a faith-filled home. Often, it's difficult for believers like Timothy to remember exactly how and when they became Christians, but it's important to pinpoint the conversion experience of confessing your sins and asking Jesus into your heart, because everyone's testimony is just as valuable as those who saw a blinding light.

Still others expect to enter heaven on their parents' faith. They're deceived by a false sense of security that they don't have to change their lifestyle or make a personal commitment to follow Christ. The Bible clarifies in John 14:6 that each of us must accept Christ as our own personal Lord and Savior. Then God wants us to share our testimony of a changed life by the glorious grace of God, and live our life in a way that attracts others to Him. Never be ashamed of how and when you found the Lord.

PERSONAL PARABLE

Publicly displayed in our home is a black and white picture of me with a group of kids at a church youth camp. This picture is a precious memory because, at the age of 12, I accepted Jesus into my heart by faith at that camp.

I had attended Sunday School for as long as I could remember, but after the murder of my highway patrolman father when I was ten, my mother renounced her faith in God and stopped going to church. However, she would send my younger sister and me to Sunday school with neighbors or drop us off at church herself.

Two years after my father's death, I attended a church youth camp where a camp counselor and the pastor's wife sat on my cot and asked, "Janet, we know you've lost your earthly father, but would you like a heavenly Father who will never leave you?" I readily said yes, and they prayed with me to accept Jesus into my heart by trusting for myself in Him. Unlike Timothy, I didn't have a believing mother, but I did have Granny Reed, whose prayers and early Bible teaching prepared my heart for accepting Jesus.

As a public speaker and author, I share my testimony, including the story of my adult rededication after 17 years of sinful backsliding. God has used my openness and vulnerability in sharing the highs and lows of walking with Him to encourage others that He welcomes into His kingdom anyone who confesses his or her sins and accepts His Son Jesus Christ, regardless of previous lifestyle and mistakes. Our history becomes His-story.

Mentoring Moment

Always be ready to share the Source of your hope and joy.

Day Four

Using Your Gifts for God's Glory

 n Paul's second missionary journey, he returned to the cities he had preached in earlier and heard about Lois and Eunice nurturing faith in the young disciple Timothy.

On Your Own and M&M's

Q: Referring to Timothy, Acts 16:2 says, "The brothers at _____ and _____ spoke _____ of him."

● Two churches—one in Timothy's hometown of Lystra and one in Iconium 20.4 miles away—speak highly of Timothy to Paul. What might young Timothy have done for believers in the next town to know about it?

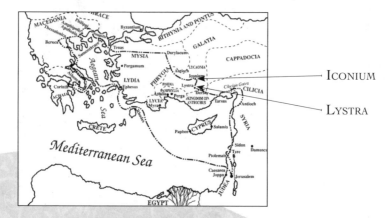

- Why would Timothy stand out from other believers?

Q: How do we know Timothy impressed Paul (Acts 16:3a)?

Q: As Paul and Barnabas experienced in Acts 13:1–3, there was a traditional laying of hands and praying over Timothy before traveling with Paul. Who laid hands on Timothy (2 Timothy 1:6)?

Q: What did Timothy receive at his "ordination"?

- 1 Timothy 1:18–19

- 1 Timothy 4:14

Q: List Timothy's spiritual gifts (2 Timothy 1:6–7; 4:2, 5).

- What was he to do with these gifts (1 Timothy 4:11–16; 2 Timothy 1:5–6)?

- For what purpose was he given them (2 Timothy 1:8–14)?

- How would putting them to use mature him spiritually?

- Who else would benefit (1 Timothy 4:16)?

Q: List practical ways to "fan the flames" of unused or undeveloped spiritual gifts.

- How confident was Timothy in using his gifts (2 Timothy 1:7)?

- Where would he gain confidence (1 Timothy 4:15–16)?

Q: Identify your spiritual gifts (1 Corinthians 12:1–11, 27–31).

- How do you use them for God's glory?

- If you're not sure of your gifts, take a spiritual gifts inventory (see p. 127).

M & M'S

Q: Mentor, describe your using mentoring gifts for God's glory.

Q: Mentee, brainstorm with your mentor ways God could use your gifts.

Q: Mentor, pray over your mentee.

FACE-TO-FACE REFLECTIONS

Paul meeting Timothy seems providential. Many who are called into ministry and service relate similar God incidences. We know that nothing happens by chance in a believer's life (Romans 8:28), and God's plan and purpose for every believer is to use his or her gifts to further the kingdom. God doesn't save us solely for our own benefit. If God is calling you to serve Him in a broader or more specific capacity, don't be afraid or timid. He will help you succeed and surround you with other believers to encourage, support, and mentor you.

PERSONAL PARABLE

In 1 Timothy 4:14 (HCSB), Paul warned Timothy, "Do not neglect the gift that is in you." On her blog (http://www.fallible.com), author Katy McKenna wrote "She Had a Book Inside Her" about her grandmother's unfinished work and hesitancy to use her gifts:

My beloved grandmother died when I was 19. It's been 38 years since I heard her say those words so many utter: "I've got a book inside of me."

I was young and naive and didn't know what she meant. The only time I ever saw her with a pencil in hand was when she was scribbling a recipe for homemade cream puffs, making a grocery list, or jotting a note of thanks or condolence to a dear friend. Then there were the letters she wrote me after I moved out of my parents' house and into my first apartment. I treasure those letters, the envelopes containing her inked thoughts, and amber newspaper clippings from the *Kansas City Star* — historical documents.

[Occasionally, I come across] these letters and inhale her scent — White Shoulders — and miss her with a grief that defies logic. I miss her wisdom, teaching homemaking skills, cooking, beautiful needlework, and the lunches of Ritz crackers, peanut butter, and a large bottle of Coca-Cola we shared so often. [Mostly,] I miss the book she didn't write. [I never asked the topic.]

I inherited so many belongings of my grandmother's but the . . . items that have disturbed me most are her unfinished projects. Since she taught me to sew, knit, crochet, embroider, and quilt, it was assumed I would complete what Grandma started. Her projects are still unfinished, languishing in my attic, waiting for . . . me?

I don't think I'll be finishing the work she began. I've finally realized a part of Grandma started all those projects to avoid the book inside of her, to keep the words locked up even while her fingers worked furiously on other beautiful projects: substitutes for her thoughts, feelings, and creativity with words.

The best I can do is use her snippets of filet crochet and random quilt blocks to decorate pillows or fashion simple doll clothes in her honor, and offer them to family members as a memorial to a treasured ancestor. And then use the rest of my life to honor her in the only other way I know how. Because, after all, I'm her granddaughter and I've got a book inside of me.

*   *   *

Mentoring Moment

Where God guides, He provides.

*   *   *

Day Five

Mentoring 101

Mentoring is teaching what someone taught you, so you can train others to teach what you taught them.

On Your Own and M&M's

Q: Second Timothy 3:14–15 (NLT) reads, *"But you must remain faithful to the things you have been taught. You know they are true, for you know you can trust those who taught you. You have been taught the Holy Scriptures from childhood, and they have given you the wisdom to receive the salvation that comes by trusting in Christ Jesus."*

● How does this verse describe a mentoring relationship?

● Who were the mentors and mentee?

● What was the mentee now prepared for?

Q: In 2 Timothy 2:1–2 (NLT), spiritual father and mentor, Paul, advises: *"Timothy, my dear son, be strong through the grace that God gives you in Christ Jesus. You have heard me teach things that have been confirmed by many reliable witnesses. Now teach these truths to other trustworthy people who will be able to pass them on to others."*

- What truths had mentor Paul taught mentee Timothy (1 Timothy 4:4–11; 2 Timothy 1:8–11)?

- Explain how 2 Timothy 1:13 and 2:2 are examples of the above definition of mentoring.

Q: What was the mentor's charge to the mentee in the following Scriptures?

- 1 Timothy 6:11–21

- 2 Timothy 2:2–3

- 2 Timothy 2:14–16

- 2 Timothy 3:14–15

- 2 Timothy 4:1–2, 5

Q: Describe how the following verses apply to mentoring and specifically to Lois, Eunice, Paul, or Timothy.

	Mentoring	Specific Application
Psalm 145:4–7		
Proverbs 13:14		
Proverbs 27:17		
John 21:15*b*		

Q: What guide did Lois, Eunice, and Paul use to mentor Timothy (2 Timothy 3:14–16)?

- What was Timothy equipped for (v. 17)?

Q: List desired characteristics of a Christian mentor.

● Who could be a mentor?

Q: What qualities should a mentee possess?

● Who might be a mentee?

Q: Suggest ways mentoring can be reciprocal (Romans 1:11–12).

● What roles did Paul and Timothy fulfill in each other's lives (2 Timothy 1:3–4)?

● Lois and Eunice?

Q: In what types of situations could someone benefit from a mentor?

● How could you benefit from a mentor or being a mentor?

M & M'S

Q: Mentor, what qualities do you see in your mentee?

Q: Mentee, what characteristics does your mentor possess?

Q: How has your relationship been two-way? If not yet, revisit this question at the end of the study.

Mentoring may be informal or an intentional, structured, committed relationship. Mentors want mentees to succeed at finding and fulfilling their life's purpose, and mentees respect their mentor's way of life and willingly learn from him or her. When seeking a mentor, look for another woman with gifts and experiences that match yours, spiritual maturity, and the ability to tell the truth in a kind and nondestructive way.

Mentoring relationships are helpful in every area of life and take various forms: discipler, spiritual encourager, coach, counselor, teacher, sponsor, contemporary model, historical model, co-mentor, and family member. Throughout our lifetime, we take on many of these roles in someone's life, and others pour into our lives in various ways. In this study, we'll focus on mentoring within the home and church family, with one generation leaving a legacy earmark for the next generation, but everything we discuss is applicable in all areas of life.

The following dialogue between my daughter Kim and four-year-old granddaughter Katelyn is a modern-day scene that could have taken place between Lois, Eunice, and Timothy in their kitchen:

Katelyn was doing her chicken scratch scribble on a big piece of paper, writing away frantically at the kitchen table.

Kim: Are you making a list?

Katelyn: No, I'm writing Noah's Ark. . . . Actually, it's a scroll.

Kim: A scroll?

Katelyn: Actually, no. It's not a scroll because it's not God's Word.

- -

PERSONAL PARABLE

Lydia Harris shares a story about two-way mentoring with her granddaughter:

Once when granddaughter Clara and I talked about the Bible, I mentioned Psalm 117 was the shortest chapter in the Bible. Clara turned to it and read aloud, "Praise the Lord, all you nations; extol him, all you peoples." She asked, 'What does *extol* mean?' Before I could think of an answer, she asked, 'Does it mean *worship*?' I wondered, *Who's mentoring whom?* We're developing a sweet mentoring relationship, and she's helping me grow up as a grandmother.

* * *

Mentoring Moment

"Mentoring takes place when divine resources meet
human needs through loving channels to the glory of God."
—Warren Wiersbe

* * *

Faith in Action

What one thing from this session does God want you to apply in your life today?

Let's Pray Together

Dear Abba, Daddy, Father, it's an awesome privilege and responsibility having children, grandchildren, family, and the family of God. We want our families and our life to glorify You. Give us boldness to share openly with others the wonders You have done in our lives and teach us how to teach others to go and do the same. There's so much for us to learn from the story of Lois and Eunice, and though the biblical words regarding them are few, the impact of their lives on Timothy has carried down through the ages. We boldly ask a blessing on our lives to have an eternal impact on our families. Amen.

NURTURING FAITH IN YOUR FAMILY

Day One

Start Young

*L*ois and Eunice have rightly been honored as model mentors for rearing children. They had a genuine faith, and they passed it on to young Timothy. We can picture the mother and grandmother, holding him as a toddler on their knees while telling Bible stories. We can imagine them guiding and correcting the growing boy with precepts drawn from Scripture. We can be sure that they prayed each day that Timothy might know the Lord and choose to serve Him."
— Sue and Larry Richards, *Every Woman in the Bible*

On Your Own and M&M's

Q: What "Holy Scriptures" would Lois and Eunice have taught Timothy (2 Timothy 3:15)?

Q: Explain how the two women lived out the following Old Testament Scriptures.
● Deuteronomy 11:18–21

● Proverbs 9:10

● Proverbs 22:6

- Isaiah 38:19

- Isaiah 54:13

Q: How would teaching and learning the Scriptures make the teachers and the student ripe for receiving the gospel when Paul came to town?

Q: Read Ephesians 6:4 and 1 Peter 3:15. Then read the humorous mother/child exchange in the Personal Parable on page 40. How do you think Lois and Eunice answered Timothy's questions?

- What reference resource would they have used (2 Timothy 3:14–17)?

- How would you answer a child's questions about heaven?

Q: What resources are available today for teaching children the Bible?

- Which ones have you used?

M & M'S

Q: Mentor, your role is to lead your mentee to the Bible when she has questions and teach her how to find answers there. You don't have to have all the answers.

Q: Mentee, don't worry if you're not familiar with the Bible; be an eager, attentive student.

When granddaughter Katelyn was four years old, she asked, "Grammie, do only girls go to heaven?" I knew this was the perfect opening to explain the gospel. We talked about death and living with Jesus forever. She asked, "Will Jesus have a bed and toys for me in heaven?" I assured her He would have everything she needed. Then I mentioned the prayer to accept Jesus into our hearts and know for sure we're going to heaven. Katelyn said pensively, "I don't know *that* prayer." I asked, "Would you like to pray it?" She eagerly said, "Yes!" I shot up a quick prayer, wondering if she was too young and if this was the right time. The Lord prompted me to continue, so I had the glorious opportunity to pray the Salvation Prayer with my little granddaughter. If I had brushed off her question about heaven, I would've missed one of the greatest joys of my life.

Lois and Eunice were Jewish women who knew the Old Testament Scriptures commanding parents to memorize God's Word and instill it into their children's minds and hearts as a part of daily life. That biblical practice is as invaluable today as it was in ancient times. Lynne Chapman, BellaOnline's Christian Living editor, writes:

> We live in an age of negative influences. God's Word has been taken out of schools and public buildings. Television and movies are full of hostility, murder, and immorality. Children can be sheltered at home but soon grow out of parental protection. In this age of negative influences bombarding children from all sides, how important it is that they receive the strong spiritual influences within the family. As mothers and grandmothers, we have a mission to build God's love into a child so that they are equipped for life.

PERSONAL PARABLE

Excerpt from "What, Me Worry? Oh, Yes" by Connie Schultz:

My overwrought nature came into full bloom when I was about 8 years old. I started grilling my mother about heaven, a state of boring bliss she assured me would last forever. The key word here: *For-evvvvvv-er.*

"What will we do there all day?" I asked.

"We won't have to do anything," Mom said as she stood at the sink and washed dishes. "It's heaven. We'll just relax."

"Relax? All day long?"

"You'll love it," she said, pausing to stare out the window. "We'll be together. With no housework."

"Well, how will we find each other?"

"People will be giving directions," Mom said, her voice starting to rise.

"What people?"

"Angels, Connie. Angels will point you in the right direction."

"So I'm going to be all alone when I get there?"

"Of course not," she said, patting our dog's head. "Shilo will be waiting for you."

"Shilo's going to die?"

That pretty much sealed it for me. Life was a long road of uncertainty.

Mentoring Moment

It's never too early to teach children that Jesus loves
all the little children of the world.

Day Two

Lay a Firm Foundation

We should love our grandchildren and children so dearly that our heart's desire is to train them to love and serve the Lord. It all starts with a firm, grounded, stable foundation in both their home life and spiritual life. *"For you, God, have heard my vows; you have given me the heritage of those who fear your name."* — Psalm 61:5

On Your Own and M&M's

Q: Describe the kind of home life Lois and Eunice would provide for Timothy.

● What challenges faced Eunice with an unbelieving husband?

Q: Titus 2:3–5 is a foundational mentoring passage. What did Paul tell Titus to teach the "older" women, and the older women to teach and train the "younger" women?

Older Women/Lois	Younger Women/Eunice
to be _____	to _____
not to be _____	to be _____
or _____	to be _____
but to _____	to be _____
	and to be _____

● Why should we do this? *"So that no one will _____ _____."*

Q: List ways the Word of God is maligned and how following Titus 2:3–5 would help:

Maligning Examples   **Titus 2:3–5 Antidote**

_____   _____
_____   _____
_____   _____
_____   _____

Q: How would Lois following Titus 2:3–5 help Eunice create a faith-filled home, even with an unbelieving husband?

Q: Read Deuteronomy 6:1–9. Lois and Eunice knew these Scriptures, so what should be the foundation and heart of their home (v. 5)? Your home?

● List ways God says to impress His commandments on children and practical applications.

Ways to Impress   **Practical Applications**
1. Talk about them when
   you sit at home   Family Bible studies
2. _____   _____
3. _____   _____
4. _____   _____
5. _____   _____
6. _____   _____

Q: How was Timothy to apply the firm foundation he received to the church he was pastoring?
● Ephesians 2:19–21 _____
● 1 Timothy 1:5 _____
● 1 Timothy 3:15 _____
● 1 Timothy 6:18–21 _____
● 2 Timothy 2:19 _____

Q: Read Luke 6:47–49 and 1 Corinthians 3:10–15. Compare family life built on a Christian foundation with one built on the world's foundation.

Q: What constitutes a foundation pleasing to the Lord (Psalm 89:14; Proverbs 3:33)?

Q: How did God lay the foundations of the world (Proverbs 3:19)?

Q: Read Proverbs 14:1. Where do we get wisdom to build firm foundations in our homes?
- Isaiah 33:5–7
- Psalm 119:11
- Hebrews 3:3–4
- James 1:5

Q: Describe a righteous home and how it compares to your home (Acts 2:45–47).

Q: If you didn't grow up in a home built on a faith foundation, what have you done differently in your home?

- Implement in your family one of the six practical applications listed above.

Q: What would your grandchildren and children say is the foundation of your life?

M & M'S

Q: Mentor, keep each other accountable in implementing the foundational applications you each chose to start in your families.

Q: Mentee, if your family life isn't built on a firm foundation, talk to your mentor about how to start the remodeling process.

Many of us grew up in homes without a firm faith foundation — or like Timothy, one or both parents weren't believers — but this isn't an excuse for not building our own homes on the foundation of Jesus Christ. If this wasn't role-modeled for you, seek out other families in church who have Jesus at the center of their home: watch and imitate what they do. Get to know the parents and suggest doing family activities together. Observe how they discipline and interact with their children and how they talk about Jesus in their home, their car, their play — all aspects of life. Ask God to help you incorporate and apply these values in your home.

PERSONAL PARABLE

"God's Children Entrusted to Us" excerpt from The Plan A MOM in a Plan B World *by Debbie Taylor Williams:*

We have a responsibility to teach our children about God, His ways, and that obedience brings blessings. How do we do that? We teach them to pray before meals, at bedtime, and in between. We teach them to have thankful hearts.

When [daughter] Lauren was little, I would take her to the window every morning, look outside, and say, "Thank You, God, for this beautiful day." I had no idea the effect it was having on her until Keith and I went out of town and left the children with their grandparents. Upon returning, one of the first stories Keith's mother told me was that Lauren went to the window, looked out, and said, "Thank You, God, for this beautiful day."

When [son] Taylor was five and Lauren was three, I asked God, "What is the greatest gift I can give my children?" He immediately impressed on my heart to give them the discipline of beginning each day with Him in prayer and Bible reading. "That way, I can take care of them all the days of their lives." My next question was, "How can I make a three- and five-year-old want to come to You first thing every morning?" Again, I felt God answer: "Kidz Time." Then He guided me to develop an easy-to-use, A-to-Z memory verse and devotional activity to do with them when they woke each morning. It was such fun! Taylor, after the fourth morning of Kidz Time, announced that he wanted to choose the verse and set up the activity for the following day. You can imagine how my heart soared. I showed him how to select a verse using the concordance in the back of his Bible. He took it from there.

You may think that once your children are out of the house, your time of teaching them God's Word has ended. Now that our children are grown, our relationship with them is one of "sharing" more than overt teaching. If you haven't been overbearing with your teaching in their childhood and have a good relationship with your adult children, you may find open doors to continue loving on your kids with the Scriptures.

● ● ●

Mentoring Moment

"If we have God's Word in our hearts, Christian teachings will flow naturally and in an encouraging way. We can help our children establish habits that will help them be dedicated to God."
—Debbie Taylor Williams, *The Plan A MOM in a Plan B World*

● ● ●

DAY THREE

*G*od has given you a unique and awesome opportunity to raise children to have a relationship with God and a life dedicated to serving Him. You are journeying and learning as a family about God's grace, love, and faithfulness through God's Word, and how to respond to life experiences."
— Mitzi Eaker, *Missions Moments 2*

ON YOUR OWN AND M&M'S

Q: After being apart, what do grandparents and parents typically bring their grandchildren or children?

● What does Paul long to give his Roman Christian family when he sees them (Romans 1:11)?

● How would a child benefit from a grandmother or mother longing to impart spiritual wealth instead of material wealth?

Q: What gifts require no money or physical presence?

Q: What did Paul constantly give his Christian family?
● Romans 1:8 _____
● 1 Corinthians 1:4 _____
● 1 Thessalonians 1:2–3 _____
● 2 Thessalonians 1:3–4 _____
● 2 Timothy 1:3 _____

Q: How did Paul, Timothy, and Silas treat the Thessalonians (1 Thessalonians 1:1; 2:7–8, 11–12), and what was the church's response (3:6)?

Q: Where would Timothy learn to treat people like a loving mother?

● A loving father and friend (1 Timothy 5:1–2)?

● To take care of Lois, probably a widow (1 Timothy 5:3–8)?

Q: Fill in the instructions to parents found in 1 Thessalonians 2:11–12 and list opportunities to apply to daily life.

Daily Life Application

E _____

C _____

U _____

Q: Describe the type of love and affection shown to children in the following verses.
● Genesis 31:55 _____
● Matthew 19:13–15 _____
● Mark 10:13 _____

Q: What might be a child's response to someone praying and praising God for him or her?

● How do you show your grandchildren and children love?

● Do you pray for them daily, and do they know it? Why or why not?

M & M'S

Q: Mentor, pray for your mentee and encourage her. While you guide, praise her for what she's doing right.

Q: Mentee, tell your mentor what makes you feel appreciated and affirmed.

Parents are responsible before God for their children's spiritual, emotional, and physical well-being for as long as they are under our control. We're also responsible before God to give children our loving and prayerful support in order to nurture them on their journey to adulthood. Seek every opportunity during daily activities and living life together to direct children to their Creator and Sustainer.

PERSONAL PARABLE

Excerpt from Preparing My Heart for Grandparenting
by Lydia E. Harris:

During his morning devotions, my husband, Grandpa Milt, reads his Bible and notes verses that apply to our family. Then he uses the verses as the basis for prayers. As he daily kneels and prays from God's Word for each grandchild, he makes an eternal impact on their lives! Seeing my husband in prayer is the dearest sight for me. After years of praying this way, he has stacks of notebooks filled with verses he has prayed. Praying from Scripture is a powerful way to influence our grandchildren's [and our children's] lives.

If our adult children are following God, we can reinforce their godly values in our grandchildren's lives. But even if our children aren't obeying God, we can still make a strong, positive imprint on our grandchildren's lives.

Mentoring Moment

"To be the grandchild of a Christian grandparent is a wonderful privilege for the grandchild and an awesome responsibility for the grandparent."
— Lee Roberts, *Praying God's Will for My Grandchild*

DAY FOUR

MAKE LEARNING FUN

 hildren are little sponges: mimics who love jingles, singing songs, and reading stories. *"May you live to enjoy your grandchildren."*
—Psalm 128:6 (NLT)

ON YOUR OWN AND M&M'S

Q: How does God rejoice over us (Zephaniah 3:17)?

Q: The Bible encourages everyone to do what children love to do—shout for joy, laugh, and make a joyful noise unto the Lord. In the following verses, "shout" in the King James Version is "joyful noise." Describe ways to implement each verse's message as a teaching moment, habit, or tradition in your family.

Family Teaching Moment, Habit, or Tradition

Psalm 66:1–3 _____

Psalm 81:1–2 _____

Psalm 95:1–2 _____

Psalm 98:4–6 _____

Psalm 100:1–2 _____

Psalm 126:2–3 _____

Q: List additional ways you joyfully celebrate the Lord in your family.

● Do all family members participate? Why or why not?

Q: Do you pray before a meal at a restaurant, or when nonbelievers are at the table? Why or why not?

● What is Paul's wise counsel (2 Timothy 1:11–12)?

Q: How do you make learning about Jesus fun for the children in your family?

M & M'S

Q: Have a joyful celebration with both of your families and implement some of the ideas from today's lesson.

FACE-TO-FACE REFLECTIONS

Making the Bible fun and easy for our grandchildren to understand and learn is a passion of mine. Gifts and the playroom at our house reinforce and nurture our family's faith. Christian bookstores and Web sites such as Christianbook.com offer an array of Christian board games, card games, DVDs, CDs, Bibles, books, computer games, clothes, and other gifts that teach children about Jesus in an age-appropriate, fun, and educational way.

My grandkids play their Christian CDs in the car, which is quite a witness to passengers. Daughter Kim's family always sings a prayer before meals, at home or eating out. Well, *almost* always. One night, company came for dinner and everyone started eating without singing the prayer. Five-year-old Brandon said, "Hey, aren't we going to sing?" Embarrassed, Mommy explained the family's customary mealtime prayer, and everyone held hands and sang the blessing.

We gave grandson Joshua a book about the armor of God and a costume to dress up in the armor, which he wore for Halloween. What a witness to the neighbors!

I love the *Quiet Time Bible for Toddlers*, which has a daily memory verse, message, and activity. While reading from this book with four-year-old Grace, her eight-year-old brother Micah ran and got his Bible and looked up all the Scriptures and read them to us.

At Christmas, we create a manger scene with hay, stuffed animals, small trees, and a trough with a Baby Jesus doll. I ordered costumes for the grandkids to dress up as Mary, Joseph, the three wise men, Gabriel, and a shepherd. We read the Christmas story, and they play the parts.

Be creative. Don't leave the spiritual education of your grandchildren and children up to Sunday School teachers and Vacation Bible School any more than you would leave discipline up to the daycare center.

PERSONAL PARABLE

Lydia E. Harris offers fun mentoring ideas:

When we invite our grandchildren for a sleepover, I pray for ways to share spiritual truths. One New Year's Eve, God gave me the idea to talk about goals starting with the letter *S*. We talked about silly goals and spiritual goals. For spiritual goals, our seven-year-old granddaughter Clara said, "Read my Bible every day."

After hearing Clara's desire, I asked her parents if I could meet with Clara twice a month for spiritual mentoring. They agreed. Recently, when I arrived to pick her up, Clara stood by the window, watching for me. A lump formed in my throat as I realized her eagerness to meet. Over pancakes and bacon, we read Joshua 1:8–9 and drew pictures in our journals to illustrate these verses.

Another time, Clara suggested we have tea with our dolls. We made scones together, and while nibbling scones and sipping tea, we talked about what the Bible says about *hospitality*, which was a new word to her. After tea, she wrote the words of Romans 12:13 in her journal.

Recently, Clara and I talked about the value of the Bible while we licked ice-cream cones. "What's the best book?" I asked Clara.

"The Bible," she quickly replied.

"What makes it the best book?" I asked.

"It's about God," she said.

● ● ●

Mentoring Moment

"I've learned that people are as happy as they decide to be."
—Anita Sherwood, mother of 8 and grandmother to 23

● ● ●

Day Five

Savor Memories

 ois was a devout Jewess who had instructed her daughter Eunice in Old Testament Scriptures, and they both instructed Timothy, who taught and instructed the next generation in the church. Lois's family passed down God's Word from generation to generation until a generation stopped making memories.

On Your Own and M&M's

Q: How did Lois live out Joel 1:2–3?

Q: How many generations does it take for something to become extinct (Judges 2:10)?

● List practices, possessions, or traditions of your parents that became extinct in your generation.

Q: How did Lois and Eunice implement the following charges to the generations?

● Esther 9:28 _____

● Job 8:8–9 _____

● Psalm 78:1–6 _____

● Psalm 145:4–7 _____

Q: Timothy was a second-generation pastor at the church in Ephesus. Describe the first-generation church in Judea (Acts 2:42–47).

● The second generation (Ephesians 2:19; 3:17–18).

● What happened to the third generation (Revelation 2:4–5)?

● How is this occurring in some churches today?

Q: What legacy and memory did King Nebuchadnezzar leave (Daniel 4:1–3)?

● In Daniel 4:4–37, how did he vulnerably share the wonders he had seen God do for him?

Q: Read Psalm 102:18. List the wonders God has done in your lifetime and specific steps to assure the memory of them doesn't fade in future generations.

Wonders God Has Performed for Me	Ways to Keep the Memory Alive

Q: How does your family make memories and preserve them for the next generation?

Q: Is there an abandoned tradition or practice in your family history you would like to reinstate? How will you bring it back?

M & M's

Q: What would you like to remember and savor about your relationship?

Q: Make a memory by serving in your church or community together. This could become a tradition.

Face-to-Face Reflections

It only takes one generation for something to become extinct and vanish. The church at Ephesus is an example of what happens when one generation doesn't pass down the love of Jesus to the next generation. The "grandparent" generation was on fire for the Lord and lived out the Christian life daily. They passed on their passion and love of the gospel to the second generation. Paul's first letter to Timothy reinforced and reminded the second-generation church of the strong foundation in Christ they had inherited from the first-generation believers.

But the second generation passed on to their children the law—outwardly how to do church—without the love—inwardly why we do church. In Revelation, the third-generation grandchildren became the church that forgot their first love. What happened to the Ephesians will happen to our generations too if we aren't cementing in the memories of our grandchildren and children our love for them, but foremost, our love for the Lord which creates a desire to obey His laws.

Personal Parable

A testimony of memories made by Debbie Taylor Williams's mother, which Debbie has passed to the next generation, as well as to generations of her readers and audiences (www.debbietaylorwilliams.com):

"In the beginning, God created the heavens and earth. The earth was formless and void, and darkness was over the face of the deep." Mama continued reading in Genesis about how God created the heavens and earth. But she did more than read the verses to me or show me a picture. To help me get a feel for what formless, void, and dark meant, she placed a brown paper grocery sack over my head and turned off the lights to make it as dark as she could that morning. I remember staring ahead of me, but there was nothing but dark. Then, we took the sack off my head and went back to the table. I was fascinated that God created life out of what had been formless and dark.

It was not the last time Mama made a spiritual impression on me. I knew I could count on finding her every morning, if not in the kitchen, sitting in her chair in the living room reading her Bible, drinking coffee, and gazing out the window as she prayed.

Mama raised my sisters and me to get ready for church on Saturday. We washed our hair, read our Sunday School lesson, filled out our offering envelopes, set out clothes, socks, and shoes. We even got our Sunday purse ready and placed it by our Bibles. There was no question: we were going to church. It was as welcome in our week as Saturday morning cartoons.

Because of Mama's spiritual influence, I dedicated my book, *The Plan A MOM in a Plan B World* to her, truly in my estimation, the greatest mom on earth.

Mentoring Moment

"As Grandmothers we are in unique positions to hand down those special items that have memories attached, whether they be material or spiritual, to those we love."
—Marty Norman, *Generation G*

Faith in Action

What one thing from this session does God want you to apply in your life today?

MODELNG
FAITH FOR
YOUR FAMILY

Day One

Family Ties

My grandparents were all about God and family. I loved spending all the time I could with them, even when they had me working, cooking, gardening, canning, and freezing. My godly grandmother's name was Grace, her only name. I told her, 'Grace was sufficient for thee.' She was the 'Queen Bee' in our family. Now, I'm taking notes from other godly grandparents and waiting for my own grandchildren."

—Renee Bishop Gowan

On Your Own and M&M's

Q: Timothy's family wasn't united in faith (Acts 16:1). Apply Paul's warning in 2 Corinthians 6:14 to (a) dating, (b) marriage, (c) other areas of life.

● How did Eunice live out 1 Peter 3:1–2?

● If your husband isn't a believer, what comfort do you derive from Eunice and 1 Corinthians 7:13–14?

Q: Describe the faith journey of the families of the following:

● Rahab (Joshua 2:1–24; 6:20–25)

- Cornelius (Acts 10:21–44)

- Lydia (Acts 16:13–15)

- The Philippian jailer (Acts 16:25–34)

Q: What role/risk did Rahab, Cornelius, Lydia, and the jailer take for the sake of her or his family?

- Whose lineage was Rahab in because of her bravery (Matthew 1:5–6, 16)?

Q: How should believers consider each other (2 Corinthians 1:1; Colossians 1:1–2; 1 Thessalonians 3:2)?

Q: How do you relate to Proverbs 18:24?

Q: Is everyone in your family "brothers"/believers? If yes, what role or risk did you take in this process, or were you the recipient of someone taking a risk?

- What current role or risk is God asking you to take with your family, and what's your response?

Q: If you haven't become a member of the family of God, are you ready now? If so, pray the Salvation Prayer on page 62.

M & M'S

Q: Share your family's spiritual history.

Q: Discuss burdens God has put on your heart for unsaved family members, and the risk or role you're willing to take in their salvation.

Q: Mentee, if you're not a believer, are you ready to pray with your mentor?

FACE-TO-FACE REFLECTIONS

Eunice became a believing Jew, and under Jewish law, a child accepted the religion of his or her mother. But under the Greek law of Timothy's father, the father dominated the home. It was probably love for Eunice and her Christ-like ways that persuaded Timothy's father to allow Lois and Eunice to nurture their new Christian faith in Timothy.

God wants the entire family to be Christ followers. This wasn't the case in Timothy's family, nor is it the norm today. Like Eunice, many women are spiritually single—married to unbelievers—or they're the only believer in the family. It can be isolating, lonely, and spiritually challenging, especially for wives trying not to usurp the husband's authority while still nurturing faith in the family. A mentor or support group provides a safe place to share concerns and obtain prayer and encouragement.

If you aren't a believer, but would like to become one, pray this Salvation Prayer or pray it with your mentor.

SALVATION PRAYER

Dear God, I have given into my sinful nature many times. I've grieved You, and Your ways haven't been my ways. Today, I want to change my life by asking Your forgiveness for my past sins and, with help from the Holy Spirit, to live a new, God-pleasing life in the future. I know I don't deserve forgiveness, but I believe You sent Your only Son, Jesus Christ, to die on the Cross for my sins, and He rose again three days later. I believe You'll forgive me and grant me eternal life. Thank You, Jesus! Help me cast off my old way of doing things and learn how to live a new life pleasing to You. And let it start today! Amen.

Now read John 3:16 and insert your name in the blanks: "For God so loved _____ that he gave His one and only Son, that if _____ believes in Him _____ shall not perish, but have eternal life."

Welcome to the family of God! Tell someone today about the joyous decision you've made to receive eternal life and live an earthly life centered on Christ. If your church has a new believer's class, join soon and/or use this study to help locate a mentor in your family, small group, church, or Christian community.

PERSONAL PARABLE

When I first became a believer at the age of 12, I had minimal family support. We had moved away from where Granny Reed lived, and she and my mother had emotionally distanced themselves after my father's tragic murder. My mother also distanced herself from God. Precious Sunday School teachers mentored and encouraged me to live a godly life. I also had the early Bible teachings of Granny Reed as a foundation and guide in my spiritual journey.

After leaving home for college, I continued to surround myself with Christian friends and attended church. However, the day after I graduated from college, I married an unbeliever, and no one counseled or mentored me regarding the consequences of an unequally yoked marriage. Five years later, I was divorced with a two-year-old daughter. God made good out of my bad choices, but today, I don't hesitate to approach a Christian woman who is considering such a marriage and share my story and the difficulties that await her.

Mentoring Moment

"Mothers write on the hearts of their children what the rough hand of the world cannot erase."
—Author Unknown

Day Two

As for Me and My House . . .

O e built harmony, goals, and vision into our children. My father had given me that purpose by saying, 'You don't know the results of your parenting until you see your grandchildren.' He set my sights long-range to build my home to see godly children growing up and creating their own families."
— Marcia Ramsland, "Wise Woman", *Tending the Soul*

"Children's children are a crown to the aged, and parents are the pride of their children." — Proverbs 17:6

On Your Own and M&M's

Q: Delineate Paul's directives on households and God's house (1 Timothy 3:4, 15).

Q: Read Joshua 24:1–31 and answer the following questions regarding Joshua sharing his faith with God's children, the Israelites.

● What did Joshua do first (vv. 1–13)?

● What must they do to serve God (vv. 14–15, 19–20, 23)?

● What was his own family's plan (v. 15*b*)?

- How did the Israelites respond (vv. 16–18, 21, 24, 31)?

- What was their reward (v. 28)?

Q: Were the Israelites successful at permanently renouncing idols? What did the Lord tell them to do (Ezekiel 14:1–6)?

Q: Read Romans 8:1–17. Verse 5 says, "Those who live according to the _____ have their minds set on what that flesh desires; but those who live in accordance with the _____ have their minds set on what the _____ desires."

- How do you keep your mind set on the Spirit and not your sinful nature?

- As a believer, you are _____ _____ , heirs of _____ (v. 16), and co-heirs with _____ (v. 17). How does that make you feel?

Q: Describe idols and "detestable practices" you've renounced as a child of God (1 John 5:19–21).

- How does the Holy Spirit help you avoid these (v. 20)?

- List any idols still lingering. Draw a line through each one as you repent and ask forgiveness.

Q: Lois and Eunice had a faith-filled home (2 Timothy 1:5). What fills your home?

Q: Read "Inviting the Relatives to Dinner" on page 67. Plan five steps to starting a Sunday supper tradition in your family:

1.

2.

3.

4.

5.

● How would this help instill and support family values?

● If extended family isn't near, who could you invite?

ON YOUR OWN

Q: How would having a mentor help you avoid giving into idols of the heart and detestable practices?

M & M'S

Q: Mentor, share with your mentee what you've renounced and how you stay faithful.

Q: Mentee, discuss with your mentor areas where you still struggle.

Q: Have a Sunday supper with your two families, and then expand it to include extended family and/or members of your church family.

FACE-TO-FACE REFLECTIONS

The world is full of enticing idols and detestable practices. We must make a conscious decision to pray before making expenditures of money, time, or energy, and ask ourselves: Does this have kingdom value? Today's advertisements bombard us from every media source with one message: You won't be happy if you don't own or experience their company's product. Consumerism is the norm in twenty-first-century life. Use the following definitions to determine if you have an idol-of-the-heart or are entertaining a detestable practice:

● Idol — anything, other than Jesus, you feel you *must* have or *can't live without*.

● Detestable practice — anything you wouldn't do in the presence of Jesus.

A Focus on the Family article, "Inviting the Relatives to Dinner," stresses the importance of establishing and passing down family customs, traditions, and values through the generations:

> In decades past, large Sunday suppers with relatives were widespread traditions: Grandma in her apron, checking on the food, the kids playing with their cousins in the yard.
>
> While times have changed, there's still value in family gatherings. Kids benefit from the love shown and the bonds forged with relatives. In today's fast-paced, often disconnected society, perhaps it's more crucial than ever to model family togetherness for your kids.
>
> If you're fortunate enough to have extended family living nearby, why not resurrect the often-overlooked tradition of a family meal? To start, consider your heritage. Prepare family recipes of the past and present — and let the children help.

The article goes on to suggest using family dinners as an outreach and opportunity to share God's love with family members who aren't yet part of God's family.

PERSONAL PARABLE

"As I think back, the best memories of my grandparents were simply spending time with us. Just being together — that's what was so dear about this evening with my own 'grands.' Horsing around, kitchen table games, telling stories, special bedtime moments of prayer and singing, 'I love You, Lord.'

Just now, I peeked in on two freshly bathed dears sleeping down the hall—I am incredibly blessed to be a Nana."
—Sharon Hoffman, author of *A Car Seat in My Convertible?*

* * *

Mentoring Moment

Godliness is caught, not taught.

What one generation tolerates, the next generation normalizes.

"Don't rush out to tell others what you're not living at home."
—Patsy Clairmont

* * *

DAY THREE

LET YOUR LIGHT SHINE

*T*he walk and witness of another widow, her mother-in-law, Naomi, won Ruth's heart, her head, and became the Bible Ruth *read* to become a believer. Ruth watched Naomi cling to her God in spite of losing all that women of that day treasured."
— Miriam Neff, "Can Anything Good Come of My Brokenness?",
Tending the Soul

ON YOUR OWN AND M&M'S

Q: What is the meaning of "let your light shine" (Isaiah 58:10; Matthew 5:15–17; 2 Corinthians 4:5–7)?

● When our light shines, who do people see in us (Galatians 1:15–16)?

Q: Read Ruth 1:1–18. Ruth grew up worshipping pagan gods. How did she learn about God (v. 16)?

● How long had Naomi and Ruth been "family" (vv. 3–4)?

● Verses 16–18 are Ruth's profession of faith. List ways Naomi must have let her light shine for Ruth to make such a commitment.

Q: In whose genealogy are Naomi and Ruth (Ruth 4:13–17)?

Q: Who let their light shine for Timothy
(2 Timothy 1:5; 3:10–11, 14–15)?

- How and to whom was Timothy to let his light shine
(1 Timothy 4:9–16; 2 Timothy 2:1–2)?

- Who, when, and how did someone let their light shine into your life?

- What were the results?

- Whose life does your light need to shine on today?

ON YOUR OWN

Q: If sharing your faith is difficult, seek out a mentor or someone from your church to give you guidelines, tips, and encouragement, as Paul did with Timothy.

M & M'S

Q: Mentor, discuss the concept of letting your light shine.

Q: Mentee, if you're a new Christian, you may be excitedly telling everyone about your newfound faith. What have the reactions been?

- Or are you embarrassed and find it hard to tell unbelievers? Ask your mentor for help.

FACE-TO-FACE REFLECTIONS

Timothy knew about God from infancy, and Ruth learned as an adult. Both had faithful family members who weren't afraid to share the Source of their hope. You and I are Christians today because someone let their light shine into our life: they took a risk and shared the good news. Or maybe like Ruth with Naomi, we saw the light shining in someone we admired: their life was a living Bible, words reflected in actions. As a Christian, others will see the light of Jesus living in you. Don't be surprised when one day someone says to you, "I want *your* God to be *my* God."

Mentoring Moment

"God's evangelistic strategy in a nutshell: He desires to
build into you and me the beauty of his own character,
and then put us on display."
—Joseph Aldrich

"Character is shown by one's habitual actions,
not the extraordinary ones."
—Kenneth Wuest

DAY FOUR

DAUGHTERS- AND SONS-OF-THE-HEART

*M*y working definition for a spiritual mothering [fathering] relationship is this: When a woman [man] possessing faith and spiritual maturity enters into a nurturing relationship with a younger woman [man] in order to encourage and equip her [him] to live for God's glory . . . please note that giving birth biologically or being of a certain chronological age are not prerequisites for spiritual mothers [fathers]."

—Susan Hunt, *Spiritual Mothering*

ON YOUR OWN AND M&M'S

Q: List terms John uses to refer to Christians in 1 John—
- 2:1, 12–13, 18, 28; 3:2, 7, 10, 18; 4:4; 5:1–2, 21

- 2:7; 3:2, 21; 4:1, 7, 11

- 2:9–11; 3:10, 13, 17; 5:16

Q: Read 1 Corinthians 4:14–16. How does Paul describe a spiritual father?

- How did Paul refer to Timothy (1 Corinthians 4:17; Philippians 2:22; 1 Timothy 1:2, 18; 2 Timothy 1:2; 2:1)?

Q: What did Naomi call Ruth (Ruth 2:2, 8, 22; 3:1, 10, 11, 16, 18)?

Q: Whose children are Christians (1 John 5:19)?

Q: Based on Susan Hunt's opening definition:
● How did Naomi spiritually mother Ruth? (Note previous day's study and Ruth 1:18–19; 2:1–3, 11–12, 17–23; 3:1–5, 18; 4:13–16.)

● How did Elizabeth spiritually mother Mary (Luke 1:35–56)?

Q: How did Paul spiritually father Timothy (2 Timothy 1:3, 13–14)?

Q: Describe someone who exemplifies a spiritual mother or father.

● What character qualities does she or he display that draws others to them?

● Do you see any of those qualities in yourself? Pick one to develop further and pray for God to develop that characteristic for His glory.

Q: In her book, *Mothers of the Bible Speak to Mothers of Today*, Kathi Macias refers to "community mothers." What situations call for a "community" mother or father?

ON YOUR OWN

Q: Are you currently in a "mother- and daughter-of-the-heart" relationship? If so, describe how it has influenced your Christian life.

● If not, where would you find a mother- and daughter of-the-heart relationship to grow spiritually and serve together?

M & M'S

Q: Is yours a "mother- and daughter-of-the-heart" relationship? Why or why not?

Q: Timothy and Paul served together to further the gospel. How might God want the two of you serving together?

FACE-TO-FACE REFLECTIONS

Spiritual mothering or *spiritual fathering* defines the type of relationship between Naomi and Ruth, Elizabeth and Mary, and Paul and Timothy. As with Ruth and Timothy, the relationship may occur when the biological parent isn't a believer, and the spiritual father or mother functions as a spiritual nurturer and Christian role model. Or perhaps one of the parents is absent from the family. Spiritual mothers- and fathers-of-the-heart don't replace the parent, but provide guidance, teaching, and discipline in the family of God.

Paul was careful to mention that Timothy had a living father, but in Paul's heart, Timothy was like a son, and they shared a special bond in Christ that Timothy didn't have with his biological father. As Paul invested time, energy, and love in Timothy, he built on the firm foundation Timothy had received from Lois and Eunice. Paul wasn't replacing family, but it was time for Timothy to receive spiritual direction from a man who could help him apply and mature in all he had learned at home. Lois and Eunice released Timothy to Paul.

Often, grandparents become mothers- and fathers-of-the-heart, or even stand-in parents raising their grandchildren. In her book, *Preparing My Heart for Grandparenting*, Lydia E. Harris tells the story of 18-year-old Courtney, who was raised in a single-parent home with a working mom. Courtney honored her grandparents on their 50th anniversary: "'Grammie, you were like a second mother to me. You led me to God. Thank you very much. You are beautiful inside and out. I want to be just like you.' She wiped tears and continued. 'Papa, you guided me and believed in me.'"

My first mentee was a young woman named Kristen. I write about our "mother- and daughter-of-the-heart" relationship in Face-to-Face with Elizabeth and Mary: Generation to Generation*:*

Kristen had a loving mom and dad, but it was difficult for her to discuss with them her spiritual questions and challenges. I had daughters Kristen's age, so when she asked me to be her spiritual mentor, we both knew that I also would be giving her a mother's perspective. The important thing for both of us to remember was that I was not Kristen's mom and she was not my daughter. Establishing that boundary allowed me to remain objective and Kristen was receptive to my advice and suggestions.

* * *

Mentoring Moment

"There is no greater pursuit or purpose to which we, as mothers, grandmothers, or community mothers can dedicate ourselves than properly training up those little ones who have been entrusted to us, teaching and modeling the only true faith and the way it should be lived on a daily basis. If we have done that, we can be sure that God will honor His word and faithfully draw our children and grandchildren into service for Him."
—Kathi Macias, *Mothers of the Bible Speak to Mothers of Today*

"I have two fathers: God in heaven and my daddy here on earth."
—Katelyn Mancini, my granddaughter, at five years old

* * *

Day Five

Follow My Example

*L*ike every Christian, Paul didn't lead a perfect life, but he did strive to live an exemplary life for others to follow. "Children would like to see that those in authority over them are also in authority to the Lord."
— Pastor Brian Smith, Crouch Community Church

On Your Own and M&M's

Q: How does John's message to parents and children in 1 John 2:13–14 echo Pastor Smith's comment above?

Q: What term describes Timothy in Acts 16:1?

● Look up the word *disciple* in the dictionary and write the definition.

Q: What is Paul's message in the following verses?

● Philippians 3:17

● 1 Thessalonians 1:6

● 2 Thessalonians 3:7

Q: Whose example was Paul following (1 Corinthians 11:1)?

● Whose example should all Christians follow (1 Peter 2:21)?

Q: Read Romans 7:15 to 8:2. What were Paul's struggles, and what example did he set?

Q: What example was Timothy to set for his followers (1 Timothy 4:12)? "Set an example for the believers in _____ , in _____, in _____, in _____ and in _____ ."

Q: List practical ways Paul specifically told Timothy to follow him. 2 Timothy—

● 1:8–9   ● 2:23–26

● 1:12–14   ● 2:15

● 2:1–2   ● 2:16

● 2:3   ● 2:22

● 2:7   ● 3:12–14

● Who else is Paul referring to in 3:14–15?

Q: In 2 Timothy 3:10, Paul says Timothy knows all about Paul's _____ _____ .

● What was Timothy to do with that knowledge (1 Corinthians 4:17)?

Q: Read Galatians 1:13–18. Describe Paul's former way of life (vv. 13–14).

● Who gave him a change-of-life experience (vv. 15–16)?

● As a new believer, whose way of life did Paul imitate (v. 18)?

Q: Read Hebrews 13:7. List those whose way of life you want to follow and imitate. (Doesn't have to be people you've met.)

Q: Fill in the blanks with your name: "Follow my _____'s example as I _____ follow the example of Christ."
● Explain how it feels saying this.

● Who's imitating your life in a good or bad way?

Q: List three areas in your life that need improving and what corrections you'll make.

Areas to Improve	Corrections to Make
1.	
2.	
3.	

Q: How will you apply 1 Timothy 4:12 to set an example in your:

Speech	Faith
Life	Purity
Love	

M & M'S

Q: Share with each other how your life today is different from your "former way of life."

Q: Mentor, are you living the life you want your mentee to follow and imitate? Why or why not?

Q: Mentee, how are you imitating your mentor?

A disciple is a follower and student of a mentor, teacher, or wise figure. All Christians are disciples and followers of Jesus Christ, and our charge is to lead lives worthy of replication. Grandparents and parents should feel comfortable saying, "Because I'm following Christ, follow me."

I often ask women, "Are you the mother today you want your daughter to become?" or, "Do you have the marriage today you want your children to have?" Children watch their parents' every move, and the parents' good and bad traits will reflect in their children — a sobering thought that parents should consider with every action taken, decision made, and word spoken.

Like Paul, you'll falter and have to ask forgiveness or admit the error of your ways, but humbleness is a good trait to model.

Susan Righetti, a dear friend of mine, shared with me a poem written by her cousin's late husband, Eugene Johnson, for her grandmother's memorial service program. The poem is titled "MAMA," which was what her children and grandchildren fondly called her, and it's signed "All Her Children." Such a tribute is what every grandparent cherishes. Susan and I also plan to write a fictional series memorializing Mama's amazing legend and legacy.

MAMA

Someone we loved passed on today
We wish we had known her longer,
She was so good to all of us
She made us feel much stronger.
She seemed to live her life for God
By being good to others,
As she considered all the world
Her sisters and her brothers.

All that we hope and pray is this
That all who knew her name,
Will take up her example
And try to live the same.
Yes, our hearts are filled with tears today
And remembering her we mourn,
But we are grateful unto God
That such a Saint was born.

All Her Children

Excerpt from an article in the Idaho Statesman *newspaper titled
"Mentor Became So Much More for Vallivue Grad":*

Dalrymple was a shy third-grader at Nampa's Central Elementary School when the Mentoring Network paired him with Bennett, a retired logger with seven grandchildren. Dalrymple plans to enter the Air National Guard and train to become an airplane mechanic. And he's grateful to the man who's been there while he developed his dreams.

"I've had a really great male role model in life," Dalrymple said.

That's what his mom was hoping for when she signed her son up for a mentor. "My son has three sisters and myself and really no guy in his life that has been there for the whole time. He's [Bennett] taught him a lot about how to be a man. When Jess would start to give up on stuff, Ray would push him to 'keep going, keep going, you can do it.'" Bennett helped him gain responsibility and confidence.

He [Bennett] says he's gained a lot from his time with Dalrymple including "the satisfaction that I might be doing something good."

The Mentoring Network executive director [added], "Kids are losing their social skills . . . They need to learn face-to-face relationship-building."

Mentoring Moment

Live your life as if someone is following your example,
because someone is.

"A student learns what his teacher knows,
but a disciple becomes what his master is."
— Robert J. Morgan

FAITH IN ACTION

What one thing from this session does God want you to apply in your life today?

LET'S PRAY TOGETHER

Dear Father, it's daunting to think of others following us and daily needing to set a good role model for them to replicate. We know in our flesh, we cannot do this on our own, but we do pray Psalm 19:14. May these words of my mouth and this meditation of my heart be pleasing in Your sight, Lord, my Rock and my Redeemer. Amen.

PARENTING
PRODIGALS

DAY ONE

WE DID THE BEST WE COULD

he genuine faith we share with our children does take root. Some faith planted in difficult soil may be slow in growing into healthy adulthood. But, watering our ministry with prayer, we can trust the God of all grace to see to it that the faith planted in children's hearts will one day flower."
—Sue and Larry Richards, *Every Woman in the Bible*

ON YOUR OWN AND M&M'S

Q: What is Paul's admonishment?

● 1 Timothy 4:12

● 2 Timothy 1:7

● 2 Timothy 2:22

● List possible *"evil desires of youth"* and contrast each with a *"righteous"* desire.

Evil Desire   **Righteous Desire**

● Pray for grandchildren or children to pursue righteous desires.

Q: A prodigal is a child who is breaking the hearts of her parents —
and of God. Summarize the defiance of these biblical prodigals
and the spiritual life of their parents.

Prodigal	Prodigal's Defiance	Parents' Spiritual Life
Cain *(Genesis 3:1; 4:16)*		
Jacob and Esau *(Genesis 25:4; 27; 33)*		
Samson *(Judges 13; 16)*		
Manasseh *(2 Kings 20; 21)*		
John Mark *(Acts 12:11–12; 12:25; 13:5–13; 15:37–39)*		

Q: Review session one, day two. What was Eunice's prodigal defiance (Numbers 36:6; Acts 16:1)?

● Speculate on Lois's reaction to her daughter's choice of a
husband.

Q: How does God categorize disobedient children?

● Proverbs 15:15

● Romans 1:29–32

● 2 Timothy 3:2–5

Q: What is God's desire for the parent/child relationship (Luke 1:17; Ephesians 6:1–4; Colossians 3:20–21)?

Q: Describe your relationship with your parents.

● With your children.

● After studying God's plan for this relationship, what changes will you make?

M & M'S

Q: If either of you have a prodigal, or were a prodigal, share as much as you feel comfortable.

● Encourage each other through this week's lessons.

FACE-TO-FACE REFLECTIONS

Eunice had her prodigal rebellion days. She knew the Old Testament Scriptures and that in her Jewish faith and culture, marrying a Greek gentile would bring disgrace to her mother. Yet even with a broken heart, Lois didn't lose heart. She maintained her relationship with Eunice, who later followed her mother's newfound faith in Christ, which Paul said in 1 Corinthians 12:13 makes no distinction between Greek and Jew: *"For we were all baptized by one Spirit so as to form one body—whether Jews or Gentiles, slave or free—and we were all given the one Spirit to drink."*

However, Paul also warned in 2 Corinthians 6:14 not to marry an unbeliever; but as God often does, He birthed good from Eunice's seemingly bad choices. The example and encouragement parents can derive from Lois's actions is to remain true to your own faith, trust that God is in control, and pray fervently and tenaciously for God's will for your wayward children.

Perhaps like Eunice and John Mark, Timothy also faltered on occasion and disappointed his faithful loving grandmother and mother, and even Paul, who admonished him not to be timid or worry about his youth and to flee youthful desires. Timothy wasn't as bold in his teaching as Paul wanted, critics easily intimidated him, and he was facing temptations. You may not have a prodigal, but every child tests his or her limits and has to learn how to navigate the path to adulthood. This session has biblical parenting tips and ways to help your child avoid trouble.

Since biblical times, there have been—and will continue to be—heartbreaking stories of faith-filled and loving parents whose children made hurtful and damaging life choices. We don't study Lois and Eunice as exceptional models of raising children solely because Timothy turned out so well, but as models of nurturing "genuine faith" in your family, even when circumstances aren't ideal.

PERSONAL PARABLE

When my daughter Kim left for college to live with her unsaved boyfriend, I was heartbroken. I pleaded with God to bring her back to Him and to me. I took full responsibility for modeling the life she was living, but I desperately wanted her to experience my renewed joy in the Lord. I couldn't live without knowing she would be with me in heaven.

Mentoring Moment

Your child's waywardness should callous
your knees, not your heart.

Day Two

Pray Daily and Persistently

O hat prompted me to pray daily was asking myself: How badly do I want my prodigal daughter to change her ways? The answer: with all my heart, I wanted Kim to repent and find her way back to God. I knew that as a praying parent, I would be working with God to accomplish that goal."
—*Praying for Your Prodigal Daughter*

On Your Own and M&M's

Q: How does God tell us to pray (Ephesians 6:18; 1 Thessalonians 5:17)?

Q: How might these Scriptures have comforted and encouraged Lois? You?

	Lois	You
● Deuteronomy 31:6		
● Psalm 119:97–105		
● Psalm 119:114		
● Jeremiah 29:11		

Q: Lois probably prayed the Scriptures for Eunice and for Timothy as he went into ministry. Personalize and pray the following Scriptures by inserting the name of your child or grandchild. Example: 1 Samuel 12:23–24—Far be it from me that I would sin against the Lord by failing to pray for __Kim__ . And I will teach __Kim__ the way that is good and right.

- Psalm 55:17
- Psalm 81:13–14
- Malachi 3:6–7
- John 8:32

- Philippians 3:13–15
- 2 Timothy 1:12
- James 5:13–16

Q: How does praying Scripture help you pray God's will instead of your will?

M & M'S

Q: Mentor, locate Scriptures to pray together that fit your personal circumstances. (Use the concordance in your Bible or www .biblegateway.com.)

Q: Mentee, praying Scripture is a good way to begin praying aloud or in a group.

FACE-TO-FACE REFLECTIONS

When kids leave for college and are exposed to coed dorms and beer parties, it's often "expected" that even the best kids will go astray. Parents rationalize: no worry, marriage and parenthood will bring them back. Parents and colleges often relinquish responsibility by accepting and rationalizing an immoral lifestyle as a "sign of the times": we can't do anything about it.

The Catholic Church has a mentoring program called Esteem for college coeds that the Christian community should consider adopting. Esteem operates from the premise that a college graduate suddenly reduced to being the young stranger in a new community and church may well grow distant or even alienated from his or her faith.

Leya, a medical student at Yale University, recalls her grandmother's parting advice as she left her Midwest upbringing: "Don't lose your faith out there on that liberal East Coast." Leya said, "I can't imagine shirking my faith, but how do you keep it important around all the chaos of med school? How do I become a meaningful member of a new parish? How do I allow the kind of experiences I've had here to continue?"

The Esteem program answers Leya's questions by placing students with a "handpicked mentor who combines professional success with religious devotion." Kathleen Byrnes, a chaplain on Esteem's executive team says about the mentors, "We wanted people who were living out a life of faith that might have struggles . . . not someone with all the answers."

PERSONAL PARABLE

When Kim decided to live with her unbelieving boyfriend at college, nothing I said or did changed her mind. Distraught, defeated, and at the end of options, I came across a little book that encouraged praying God's Word back to Him for your child. That was something I *could* and *would* do faithfully, even when I didn't see any changes in her. God was working in heaven, and as a parent, my job was to partner with Him on Earth. It took five long and painful years of daily praying biblically, expectantly, persistently, sacrificially, unceasingly, and thankfully, until at last, she returned to me and then to the Lord.

I also prayed for God to surround Kim with godly people who would challenge her and convict her to change her ways. I still pray that for her today. While she loves the Lord and raises her children in a Christ-centered home, peers have a strong influence at any age, and the temptations of this world are strong.

Mentoring Moment

The Holy Spirit intercedes when you don't know what to pray. He hears the cries of your heart. Christian grandparents and parents have an indisputable obligation to pray for their grandchildren and children, consistently and persistently.

Day Three

Love Unconditionally

*U*nconditional love doesn't come easy when children are rebelling against our values and everything we've taught them. Loving isn't an emotion, it's an action.

On Your Own and M&M's

Q: With a prodigal, quarrelling may come more naturally than loving. What does Paul counsel (2 Timothy 2:23–26)?

Q: Read 1 Corinthians 13:4–7. List elements of love and corresponding ways to display this kind of love to a prodigal.

Elements of Love	Display to a Prodigal
_____	_____
_____	_____
_____	_____
_____	_____

Q: What three things will outlive us (1 Corinthians 13:13)?

● Which is the greatest?

Q: What does genuine love look like (Romans 12:9–10; 1 John 3:16–20)?

Q: Describe the "children" Christ died for (Romans 5:6–8).

● What were we *all* before accepting Christ?

Q: Where will parents get the wisdom and strength to show unconditional love (Philippians 4:13)?

Q: How does Ephesians 4:15 and 2 Timothy 2:25–26 instruct us to speak?

● Give an example of admonishing in love.

● Encouraging in love.

Q: Who needs your unconditional love today?

M & M'S

Q: Mentor, if either of you are struggling with showing unconditional love to a family member, discuss ways to take the first step and keep each other accountable.

FACE-TO-FACE REFLECTIONS

Loving unconditionally doesn't mean allowing someone to hurt or abuse you, nor does it mean reconciling with a harmful or dangerous person. What it does mean is a change of heart: *"For out of the overflow of the heart the mouth speaks"* (Matthew 12:34). Instead of resenting or thinking poorly of the person, we see them the way God does: someone who needs redemption and forgiveness. We'll talk more about forgiveness tomorrow, but the groundwork for loving someone in spite of their behavior starts with our own attitude.

I grew up with a mother who showed love when I did things that pleased her and removed love when I disappointed her. Lois maintained a close, loving relationship with Eunice, maybe even living with her, even after Eunice married out of her faith and culture. When my daughter was in her prodigal years, I didn't condone her behavior, but I didn't condemn her. She knew I didn't approve of her lifestyle, but she also knew this didn't affect my love for her.

PERSONAL PARABLE

Today, many loving grandparents are raising their grandchildren because of prodigal parents. Ann shares how her grandparents' unconditional love, even during her own prodigal years, sustained her and gave her a future:

I grew up with my grandparents and I remember wonderful times. They adopted my older sister and me when I was six months old and our parents were going to put us in a home. My grandfather went to heaven when I was ten, so that left my grandmother to raise us, but she had Christian friends and her church to help.

My sister grew up rebelling and resenting our parents for giving us up, but I was thankful God got us out of that situation and put us with godly grandparents. When I was 12, we moved. My sister and I weren't happy. I didn't like school anymore and went from an A student to dropping out. Later, I wished I had finished school and went back to get my GED.

My grandparents were so good to us and loved us through all our good and bad years. Today I'm a Christian, worshipping at the same church since I was 18, and have my CDA in early childhood education and work at a daycare, which I love.

Mentoring Moment

"I don't have to arm wrestle my daughter back to Jesus.
I love her—and let God handle the rest."
—Patricia Raybon, *Praying for Your Prodigal Daughter*

Day Four

Practice Forgiveness

 *ord, if you keep in mind our sins then who can ever get an answer to his prayers? But you forgive! What an awesome thing this is!"*
— Psalm 130:3–4 (TLB)

On Your Own and M&M's

Q: How would the following verses have helped Lois forgive Eunice and help you forgive someone?

	Lois	**You**
Proverbs 10:12		
Matthew 6:12, 14–15		
Matthew 18:21–22		
Luke 17:3–4		
Ephesians 4:31–32		
Philippians 4:8–9		

Q: Forgiveness is a choice, the same choice God made to forgive us our sins. What do you learn from the following verses?

- Jeremiah 31:33–34
- John 8:1–11
- Ephesians 4:2, 22–27

Q: How does God forgive us (Psalm 103:2–4, 8–10)?

He is
C_____ and _____ .
Slow to _____ .
Abounding in _____ .
T _____ us as our sins _____ or
R _____ us according to our _____ .

Q: How great is God's love for us (Psalm 103:11–12)?

Q: What is the comparison in Psalm 103:13?

Q: How far-reaching is God's love and forgiveness (Psalm 103:17)?

● Describe how being forgiven feels.

Q: Who needs your forgiveness, and from whom do you need to ask forgiveness?

● Where will you gain the strength and courage?

M & M'S

Q: Mentor, guide the forgiving and asking for forgiveness process.

FACE-TO-FACE REFLECTIONS

When Eunice gave birth to Timothy, Lois must have focused on God's gift rather than her disappointment with Eunice's marriage. Accepting Timothy's father and forgiving Eunice may have been the first fruits of Lois becoming a Christian.

In my Bible study, *Face-to-Face with Euodia and Syntyche: From Conflict to Community*, I discuss unconditional forgiveness—forgiving without expecting anything in return:

Forgiving unconditionally means never taking it back! We may have to forgive the same person repeatedly for new offenses, but each incident is a new act of forgiveness. Even if the other person denies, excuses, or becomes offended, that doesn't influence our decision to forgive.

Forgiveness is vertical between you and the Lord and it sets your heart free from the sin of bitterness. Reconciliation is horizontal between you and the other person. Forgiveness must accompany reconciliation, but reconciliation may not follow forgiveness if the other person presents a danger or is unwilling to reconcile.

PERSONAL PARABLE

Like Eunice, Sharron married an unbeliever, even when she knew better, and the "Lois" in her life chose to look for the good from a forgiving heavenly Father:

I was a Christian who didn't trust my God enough to be obedient and made the decision to ignore His Words about marrying outside my faith. My future husband was a good man, but not a Christian. When he called his beloved Texas grandmother, she asked to speak to me. Her first words in her thick Southern drawl were, "Darlin' . . . all I need to know is . . . are you a Christian?" Surprised, I replied, "Yes, I am." This precious old woman broke into tears and told me she'd been praying all his life (he was 33 years old and never married) that he would marry a Christian woman.

We married with her blessing, and God forgave my disobedience and brought my husband into a relationship with Him. Now I know we'll both meet "Nanny" in heaven.

• • •

Mentoring Moment

"We must forgive our prodigals even if they never repent.
It will destroy us if we don't."
— Chris Adams, *Praying for Your Prodigal Daughter*

• • •

DAY FIVE

DON'T GIVE UP!

y dear friends, if you know people who have wandered off from God's truth, don't write them off. Go after them. Get them back and you will have rescued precious lives from destruction and prevented an epidemic of wandering away from God."

—James 5:19 (*The Message*)

ON YOUR OWN AND M&M'S

Q: What is the message of Malachi 4:5–6, the last words of the Old Testament?

Q: Read Proverbs 1:1–7. List ways that reading a Proverb daily would make you a wiser parent:

1.

2.

3.

4.

5.

6.

Q: Lois and Eunice epitomized Proverbs 22:6 and Timothy did go the right way. What gives hope to a parent whose child has gone astray?

- 1 Chronicles 17:16–20

- Lamentations 3:26

- John 3:16

- Romans 8:24–28

- 1 Thessalonians 1:3

- 1 John 4:4

Q: Even when it seems a prodigal may never return, what does Nehemiah 4:14 and Romans 12:12 encourage grandparents and parents?

Q: Paraphrase and personalize—as it applies to your prodigal—Hebrews 11:1.

Q: Read one chapter in Proverbs each day for a month and journal the experience.

M & M'S

Q: Commit to the daily reading and journaling of Proverbs and discuss the experience.

Q: Encourage each other when you want to stop or give up.

FACE-TO-FACE REFLECTIONS

There's always the possibility of a prodigal not returning—at least not in your lifetime—but the Lord asks you to faithfully pray and trust Him. Knowing that God wanted my daughter back more than I did comforted me. Most grandparents and parents attest that even if there's no change of heart in the child they're praying for, there's a change in their own hearts.

After Kim finally turned around after five years of diligently praying for her daily, the pastor praying with her to accept Christ told me that while he was the fortunate person present at the glorious moment, the persistent prayers of the parents paved the way!

Parents often tell me their frustrations, disappointments, and discouragements with their prodigals. I answer everyone the same way I sign every *Praying for Your Prodigal Daughter* book: "Don't give up! Keep Praying!"

Aren't you glad God didn't give up on you?

PERSONAL PARABLE

Praying and waiting mom, Robin, shares her story in
Praying for Your Prodigal Daughter:

Waiting on the Lord has proven to be one of the best things I could do for my two prodigal daughters, my marriage, and my life. Daily I'm learning to practice surrendering by being a godly example of a wife and mother. My life is now rooted in the truth of His Word, and I live on His promises daily. I believe all things are possible through Christ because I'm living proof that He is who He says He is—my Redeemer, Savior, and Lord of my life—and one day He will be that for my prodigal daughters too, when they choose to turn to Him. He'll be waiting—just before they return to me with their whole hearts. What a glorious thought!

Mentoring Moment

When Senator Mark Hatfield toured Calcutta,
he asked Mother Teresa, "How can you bear the load
without being crushed by it?" Her reply: "My dear Senator,
I am not called to be successful, but faithful."

• • •

FAITH IN ACTION

What one thing from this session does God want you to apply in your life today?

LET'S PRAY TOGETHER

Oh, Father, our hearts break when our children choose a path so far from Yours and ours. Lord, we feel like failures and we fear for what might happen to our precious child. Protect her, Lord; keep him safe. Help us to pray Your will and not our own. Open the door of her heart; cast Satan out of his life. Help us love our grandchildren and children unconditionally, as we know You do. Amen.

RAISING UP THE NEXT GENERATION IN THE CHURCH FAMILY

DAY ONE

RECOGNIZING YOUNG LEADERS

The second letter to Timothy contained Paul's last mentoring words. Paul knew about Timothy's youth, his weaknesses, and the difficulties facing the church, but he also saw potential in an ordinary person, like you and me—even committing the mission and future of the church to a shy, retiring, timid, sincere but uncomfortable with opposition, faith-filled young man.

"Yet Christ's church has endured and, from generation to generation, communicated the life that is our Savior's enduring gift to those who choose to make Him their own. How important then Paul's last words to Timothy would be. They comfort us ordinary people, and give us guidelines for maintaining the church of Jesus Christ as His living, growing family."

— Lawrence O. Richards, *The Teacher's Commentary*

ON YOUR OWN AND M&M'S

Q: In 1 Timothy 4:12 (NLT), Paul still referred to Timothy as a *"young disciple"* approximately 15 years after Timothy started traveling with him, so Timothy went into ministry as a teenager. How are young leaders sometimes received (1 Corinthians 16:10–11; 1 Timothy 4:12)?

Q: Read Acts 13:13 and 15:36–41. Describe the scenario with young John (Mark) and Paul.

- Paul met Timothy shortly after refusing to take John Mark. What impressed Paul about Timothy (Acts 16:1–3)?

- How effective was Paul and Timothy's ministry (Acts 16:4–5)?

Q: What was important to Paul in a potential leader and worker for Christ?

- Romans 5:3–4

- 2 Corinthians 12:12

- 2 Thessalonians 1:4

- 2 Thessalonians 3:5

- 1 Timothy 4:16

Q: What analogy did Paul use for leadership and ministry (Acts 20:24; 2 Timothy 4:7)?

Q: Young leaders can make mistakes and disappoint. Who mentored John Mark (Acts 15:39)?

Q: What evidence proves Paul didn't give up on John Mark, the author of the Second Gospel?

- Colossians 4:10

- 2 Timothy 4:11

- Philemon 24

Q: Timothy knew Old Testament Scriptures. Read Psalm 71:5–8 as a possible prayer from Timothy when he launched his ministry with Paul. (Insert Timothy [T] and Eunice [E].)

For you have been my T_____'s hope, Sovereign LORD, my confidence since my youth. From birth I T_____ have relied on you; you brought me forth from my mother E_____'s womb. I T_____ will ever praise you. I T_____ have become a sign to many; you are my strong refuge. My mouth is filled with your praise, declaring your splendor all day long.

- Insert the name of your grandchild or child and his or her mother.

Q: What might Lois and Eunice have thought about Timothy becoming Paul's protégé?

- Dialogue a conversation with Eunice persuading her husband to allow this opportunity.

Q: Discuss your thoughts regarding a grandchild or child following his or her dream or calling.

Q: Describe a time in your youth when someone saw your potential. How were you encouraged, and how did it change your life?

ON YOUR OWN

Q: Where would you find a young protégé to mentor and encourage?

M & M'S

Q: Investigate youth organizations to serve in together.

FACE-TO-FACE REFLECTIONS

When I reconnected on Facebook with Maria, a former mentor in Saddleback's Woman to Woman Mentoring Ministry, I was delighted to learn that she was still mentoring: "I'm using my 'mentoring skills' to help raise up the younger women in the church choir who will be leading when my generation steps aside."

Paul mentored many young leaders: some like Silas already had influence and leadership skills (Acts 15:22); others like Timothy and Titus were Paul's homegrown converts; still others, like John Mark, didn't catch on as quickly as Paul wanted. Regardless of his protégés' backgrounds, Paul saw potential for them serving in his ministry and carrying on his work after he was gone. Paul poured everything he knew into young men who shared his passion for spreading the gospel (2 Timothy 4:6). He understood: the greatest legacy isn't our accomplishments; it's our *protégés'* accomplishments.

Mentoring Moment

"Leaders are not mass produced, but must be mentored one at a time. The greatest contribution a leader can make is to develop more leaders. Young leaders can influence by their example, if nothing else."
—John C. Maxwell, *The Maxwell Leadership Bible*

"If we're going to pass down the legacy to the younger generation, we *must* mentor."
—Chris Adams, LifeWay women's ministry senior specialist

Day Two

Developing an Apprentice

*P*aul suffered much duress and persecution during his ministry (2 Timothy 1:8–12). Writing 2 Timothy from prison, he understood the gravity of nurturing young leaders in the faith to take his place and carry on his work. Because of the solid foundation and training provided by the team of Lois and Eunice, he selected Timothy as one of those fortunate apprentices and recipients of teaching, training, and mentoring in preparation for that day.

On Your Own and M&M's

Q: How did Jesus send out His disciples when they were in training (Mark 6:7; 14:13)?

Q: Read Acts 9:1–28; 11:25–30. Who apprenticed Paul (called Saul), and did they travel alone or together?

● What did Paul do with his apprentices (Acts 15:40–41; 16:3–4; Galatians 2:1–3)?

● How did Paul send out his disciples (Acts 19:22)?

Q: Follow the progression of Timothy's roles and responsibilities in Paul's ministry:

Role and Responsibility

- Acts 17:14–15

- Acts 19:22

- Acts 20:4

- Romans 16:21

- 1 Corinthians 4:17

- Philippians 2:19–24

- 1 Thessalonians 3:1–2, 6

- 1 Timothy 1:2

Q: What do the following church greetings reveal about Timothy's "on-the-job training"?

- 2 Corinthians 1:1
- Philippians 1:1
- Colossians 1:1
- 1 Thessalonians 1:1
- 2 Thessalonians 1:1

Q: Paraphrase the premise of Ecclesiastes 4:8–10.

Q: Describe Eunice's role as a younger apprentice to the older, wiser matriarch, Lois.

Q: How can mothers and daughters, fathers and sons, have an "apprentice" relationship, and how is this preparation for adulthood?

M & M's

Q: Mentor, do you consider your mentee an apprentice? If not, list ways she could "come alongside you" in life and ministry. What could you do *two-by-two*?

Q: Mentee, tell your mentor something you'd enjoy doing with her.

FACE-TO-FACE REFLECTIONS

In my book, *The Team That Jesus Built*, I wrote, "Apprentices learn by assisting the person to whom they are apprentices. They're ready to step in and take those women's places if and when necessary. With this *two-by-two* method, team members don't experience burnout because they're sharing the workload. If a team member vacates a position, there's no gap in service: someone trained and ready steps into the position."

Paul followed Jesus's example and humbly started giving away his ministry to future leaders, who followed their leader and trained leaders who went on to do the same.

Lois and Eunice supported each other and worked together in raising Timothy. When Lois passed away, Eunice would be capable of carrying on what she had learned from her godly mother.

PERSONAL PARABLE

A man in our community builds beautiful hand-carved log furniture and cabins from trees he chops down. When asked how he learned this unique trade, he replied, "I learned this from my dad, who learned it from his father." I can imagine the young boy as an apprentice at his dad's workbench: asking questions, helping dad, and eventually making his own projects. A craft that comes so easily to him as an adult had a learning curve requiring patience and persistence from both parties.

The son's son is not building log furniture; he's an apprentice in another trade. Our grandchildren and children may not follow our chosen career or venture, but we pray they will follow the Master Carpenter, Jesus Christ.

• • •

Mentoring Moment

"If you want to go fast, go by yourself.
If you want to go far, go with others."
—Rick Warren

"Churches need leaders who have the skills to equip
others to team with them in ministry."
—C. Gene Wilkes

• • •

Day Three

Training, Equipping, Commissioning

As a loving father in the ministry, Paul gave thoughtful advice to young Timothy. He reminded Timothy of his legacy of faith from his grandmother Lois and his mother Eunice. Then, in this [2 Timothy] final letter, Paul gave Timothy direct instruction. His advice was to affect Timothy's attitude and actions. The loving counsel of Paul to Timothy is timely advice to Christians today."

—Dorothy Kelley Patterson and Rhonda Harrington Kelley,
Women's Evangelical Commentary

On Your Own and M&M's

Q: Paul gave instructions regarding specific areas of ministry. What are they, and how would Timothy's upbringing help him understand and implement them? 1 Timothy—

	Area of Ministry	Upbringing
1:3–11		
2:1–15		
3:1–16		
4:1–16		
5:1–3		
6:3–11		
6:20–21		

Q: Read 1 Timothy 5:21–22 and 6:11–16. What charge did Paul give to Timothy?

● How is it possible to serve "without spot or blame"?

Q: Second Timothy records Paul's pastoral commissioning of Timothy. Patterson and Kelley from the opening quote call this letter "Paul's Be-attitudes to Timothy." Draw a line from the Scripture to the matching "Be-attitude." Next to each "Be-attitude," write the name of a grandchild or child you want to encourage with the message.

2 Timothy	Be-attitude	Child or Grandchild
1:3–7	Be strong in grace	_____
1:8–12	Be true to God's Word	_____
1:13–18	Be filled with God's grace	_____
2:1–13	Be thankful for God's blessings	_____
2:14–26	Be bold with the gospel	_____
3:1–9	Be a diligent worker	_____
3:10–17	Be determined to fulfill your ministry	_____
4:1–8	Be wary of false teachers	_____
4:19–22	Be loyal to the faith	_____

Q: How are you preparing the young people in your family for commissioning into a world not always friendly toward Christians?

● Were you prepared in your home?

● Describe your transition into adulthood.

M&M'S

Q: Plan a "commissioning" ceremony for the closure of your mentoring relationship.

Q: Mentee, you may remain close to your mentor, but be ready to become a mentor someday yourself.

FACE-TO-FACE REFLECTIONS

First and Second Timothy and Titus are the Pastoral Letters because they provided his apprentices with instructions for pastoring a church and confirmed to the congregations that these new young pastors had the same authority as Paul. He had trained and equipped them with what I call "Empowerment Steps." They
● traveled on missions trips with Paul.
● were sent as apostolic representatives to churches.
● worked as "co-workers" side-by-side with Paul.
● were left in charge while Paul went on missionary journeys.

Now realizing that he was at the end of his earthly ministry, Paul released Timothy and Titus to continue his work by granting them responsibility, authority, and encouragement, an essential aspect of commissioning. Paul wanted the next generation of pastors to succeed. He provided written instructions and guidelines to refer to when doubts flooded their minds and souls.

It's vital that successful pastors today continuously pour wisdom and experience into the next generation of leaders and pastors, preparing them to continue the work of the church. There is no greater tribute.

PERSONAL PARABLE

As the school year commenced, Larry, the worship director at Crouch Community Church, shared with the congregation a thank you card from Carolyn, a high school student who had grown up in the church and was now heading for college. Larry said he remembers Carolyn as a little girl, and before receiving the thank you note, didn't realize the impact this small-town church had on her. Her handwritten words are a testimony to the mentoring this church had provided Carolyn:

I would like to thank the congregation of the Crouch Community Church. Many of the members here are like family offering love, support, and prayers. I look up to and greatly admire the people I have met at church. I want to thank all of you for your positive influence in my life.

I look forward to the next chapter of my life. I am so lucky to have a solid relationship with God and friends here I can always call on. I know no matter what future challenges I face in "the real world," I'll always have my faith to rely on. It gives me so much confidence and strength.

Thank you from the bottom of my heart for everything.
Love, Carolyn

Mentoring Moment

"Church and home are character-building havens."
— Pastor Brian Smith, Crouch Community Church

DAY FOUR

PASSING THE TORCH AND BATON

*L*ois played a great role in the lives of her daughter and her grandson,' wrote Ranie Yesudian, a grandma from India. 'Her faith was like an Olympic torch passed on from generation to generation.' Timothy's grandmother, Lois, and his mother, Eunice, planted seeds of God's Word in his young heart, preparing him to see his need for a Savior. One of the reasons that Timothy could firmly believe the truth of God's Word was because of the credibility of the messengers—'knowing from whom you learned it.' When children and grandchildren see the truth and grace of Christ worked out (although imperfectly) in us, they often want to believe in Him, too. By God's grace, we can do that for future generations."

—Ellen Banks Elwell, *The Christian Grandma's Idea Book*

ON YOUR OWN AND M&M'S

Q: How did Jesus pass the torch to His disciples?

● Matthew 28:16–20

● Mark 16:15, 19–20

● Luke 24:50–51

Q: Describe Paul's passing of the torch in 2 Timothy 2:2 and 4:6–8.

Q: What emotions might Lois and Eunice experience as Timothy carried on Paul's work?

● While proud, what might they also fear (Acts 14:19; 2 Timothy 1:8; 2:3; 3:11–12; 4:14–15)?

● What greater purpose would they need to embrace (2 Timothy 1:9–12; 2:7–13)?

● Read 1 Samuel 1:28. How could Hannah's prayer comfort them?

Q: With responsibility comes sacrifice. Describe the metaphors in 2 Timothy 2:3–7 and the ministry service application.

Metaphor	Application
1.	
2.	
3.	

Q: List the points in Paul's final charge to Timothy (2 Timothy 4:1–2, 5):

1.	5.
2.	6
3.	7.
4.	8.

● What would help Timothy implement these (2 Timothy 3:16)?

● Where did Timothy learn the Word (1 Timothy 4:6; 2 Timothy 3:14–15)?

Q: What was Paul's—and probably Lois and Eunice's—long-term goals for Timothy (1 Timothy 1:18–19; 2 Timothy 4:7–8)?

Q: Would Paul's last words be encouraging or discouraging to timid Timothy (2 Timothy 4:16–18)? Why?

Q: What has God entrusted to you that He wants passed on to others in your family and the family of God?

● Who could you train to serve God?

Q: Outline action steps for being a Paul and finding your Timothy.

● Being a Lois or Eunice to a family member.

Q: Who do you love and treasure enough to release to God's will?

● Pray 2 Timothy 1:12 for him or her: "Lord, I am convinced that You are able to guard what I entrust to You. I commit my children to You and thank You for Your protection and care."

M & M'S

Q: Mentor, ask your mentee where she feels God is calling her to serve. Is she ready to be a mentor, and who is your next mentee?

Q: Mentee, at some point, the student becomes the teacher. Look for a younger Christian to teach what you've been taught.

FACE-TO-FACE REFLECTIONS

It's heart-wrenching letting go of our children, whether into ministry, marriage, college, career, military—wherever life takes them away from the comfort and security of home. It's just as hard to say, "Lord, here is my child. I give him or her back to You to do Your will." But

Face-to-Face with Lois and Eunice

nothing compares with the heart-swelling jubilation of knowing that your child is a follower of Christ; and it's an added blessing if, like Timothy, he or she chooses to serve the Lord—a parent's "well done, my good and faithful servant."

Following is an excerpt from the blog of Peter Grant, student pastor of Mikado Student Ministry, titled "Passing the Baton":

> Every effective leader understands the importance of passing the baton to the next generation. Early in the ministry of the apostle Paul he took on a young assistant, a man named Timothy, and he mentored him to be the one who would carry on the work after Paul was gone.
>
> My burden is for the next generation to have the baton of faith passed to them so that [they] may succeed in the eyes of God. The responsibility lies on our shoulders. Parents, older siblings, teachers, and friends this challenge is for each one of us. Who will stand in the gap and be a spiritual leader?
>
> Timothy was a success by God's grace and by Paul's guidance.

PERSONAL PARABLE

Pastor Ray Ortlund and his wife, Anne, ministered and mentored for more than 50 years, and together, they founded Renewal Ministries. I had the privilege of knowing both of these ministry giants, who each mentored a group of "disciples" annually. A requirement for being in their mentoring groups was a commitment to pass on what you learned to another group of disciples. I was one of Anne's "disciples" and gladly discipled my own groups, teaching what Anne had taught me.

After Ray's passing, Anne passed the baton of Renewal Ministries to their son, Pastor Ray Ortlund Jr., and his wife, Jani, who each also have weekly discipleship groups. In their June 2011 Renewal Ministries newsletter, Ray Jr. wrote this Father's Day tribute to his dad:

Many of you knew my own dad. He was the most magnificent man of God I have ever known—radiant with the likeness of Jesus, tenderhearted to all he knew, faithful in pressing the gospel forward in his generation. Dad was theologically careful, but not heavy-handed with it. He was loving and generous, but not sentimental. He was enthusiastic for revival, but he let the Lord work the miracles. He was ruggedly obedient to God, but cheerful. My dad was, as the Bible says, "thoroughly equipped for every good work" (2 Timothy 3:17).

How we miss Dad! But the Lord has us here now, running forward with the baton of Renewal Ministries which dad and mom graciously passed to us, continuing the work Jani and you and I all feel so passionately about—renewal today for sinful people, exhausted people, defeated people, whom God loves so wonderfully in Christ!

As we come now to Father's Day, let's honor God our Father, above all others, by giving ourselves fully to Him for His glory in our generation!

Mentoring Moment

"My mom was truly the godliest woman I know. Her love for and sharing of God's Word was her passion and my legacy."
—Philis Boultinghouse, senior editor, Howard Books

DAY FIVE

MENTORING IS NOT AN OPTION

istory is not dust. Nor is it myths we tell to comfort and acquit ourselves. Nor is it a lever we twist in order to gain political advantage. No, our history is the master narrative of who we are. And we allow all that to be forgotten at our own peril. How can our children write the next chapter of a story they don't even know?"

—Leonard Pitts Commentary in *Idaho Statesman*

ON YOUR OWN AND M&M'S

Q: Lois and Eunice honored Deuteronomy 4:9–10. How do you?

Q: Meditate on Psalm 71:17–18. What have you seen the Lord do? Have you told the next generation? Do they know the Bible? Have you turned your life lessons into lessons for them? If yes, how? If no, why not?

● How will you "never forget" the wonders of God?

● What will you do to ensure your grandchildren and children never forget?

Q: Read Psalm 78:1–8. We are to remember God's Word and His wonders, and like Lois and Eunice, tell them to the next generation so they will:
1. v. 7*a*
2. v. 7*b*
3. v. 7*c*
4. v. 8

Q: Make a list of the things you've seen God do during this study and share that list with your family and friends.

Q: How did Paul describe the end of his life (Philippians 2:17; 2 Timothy 4:6)?

● Who did Paul want with him (2 Timothy 4:9)?

Q: Into what or whom are you pouring out your life?

M & M'S

Q: Plan a combined gathering of your families, including any grandchildren and children, and share the wonders you've seen God do in your relationship.

Q: In session one, you considered the reciprocity of your relationship. How would you answer that question today?

FACE-TO-FACE REFLECTIONS

Luke Russert, son of the legendary TV journalist Tim Russert who died suddenly on Father's Day 2008, wrote an article about his father titled "Lessons from My Father." The younger Russert who, like his dad, became a Capitol Hill correspondent for NBC News applies Dad's mentoring lessons, on and off the job. Luke wrote about his father: "He was not only my best friend, but my compass. While he was alive, he guided me with his actions and advice. Since he's been gone, those 'lessons of life,' as he once called them, have continued to give me counsel and comfort."

The lessons of life Luke referred to sound much like the ones Paul gave to Timothy:

1. Believe that you can do it!

2. It's OK to be scared, but acknowledge your fears and understand them—you might need help, but you can overcome them.

3. Remember the little things and give selflessly of yourself.

What every mentor, mother, father, grandparent, and community parent should add to Tim Russert's advice to his son is that you can do all of these things through Christ who gives you strength in your weakness.

PERSONAL PARABLE

Joanne Schultz made the choice to become a "community mentor mom":

My heart stirred when I read a plea in the church bulletin for someone to help a mom with newborn quadruplets. I wasn't looking for anything to add to my already busy days. I had raised a blended family of seven children and now had an empty nest and was a grandmother. I wasn't crazy about helping raise someone else's children, but how could I not respond? How could I ignore such a desperate cry when I knew I could help—even if just a little while each week. It wasn't even an option not to become involved.

Answering the plea, I've continued going one afternoon each week, month after month. The quads are now three years old and Mommy and I have developed a close relationship. She shares with me the frustration of life as the mom of quads and dreams for her family and herself. I treat her as I would my own daughter, and since her own mother is deceased, she has come to think of me as her "mentor-mom."

I wish I could solve her problems and fulfill her needs, but I can't. I try to answer her many questions—some as simple as how to prepare a particular food for dinner—others more serious and difficult to answer. Often I have to say, "I don't know, honey. We'll have to keep praying about it."

Mentoring Moment

"Whether we dip into the prophets, the psalms, or the epistles, a couple of principles keep surfacing: *Remember God's Word and God's wonders and tell them to future generations.*"
—Ellen Banks Elwell, *The Christian Grandma's Idea Book*

"When my life is over, there's nothing more I'll be judged on than what kind of father I was."
—Tim Russert, NBC News's Washington bureau chief and former moderator of *Meet the Press*

"I'll let you in on the sweet old truths, stories we heard from our fathers, counsel we learned at our mother's knee. We're not keeping this to ourselves, we're passing it along to the next generation—God's fame and fortune, the marvelous things he has done."
—Psalm 78:2–4 (*The Message*)

FAITH IN ACTION

What one thing from this session does God want you to apply in your life today?

LET'S PRAY TOGETHER

Lord, it's a huge responsibility leaving a legacy for the next generation and assuring they're ready to carry on in our place. Keep us humble—remembering that once we were young and so appreciative of mentors willing to share pieces of their life with us. You now tell us to go and do the same. Thank You for everyone who poured into us, and now, Lord, use us where You will to impact the kingdom of God for generations to come. Amen.

A Granddaughter's Good-byes, Blessings, and Regrets

by Kathy Howard, author of Unshakeable Faith

Today, I said good-bye to my last grandparent. My father's mother, Verna Sumner Head Boyd Moses McGraw Jones, died at 103. She lived a lot of life. She buried four husbands. She saw many changes in the ten decades she walked this planet. As my preacher cousin pointed out today, the year she was born, Henry Ford introduced the Model A automobile.

Today blessed me in a number of ways. I got to hug and visit with cousins, aunts, and uncles I haven't seen in many years. Some I didn't even recognize. My grandmother had 8 children, 18 grandchildren, 38 great-grandchildren, and even a few great-great-grandchildren.

For the last two days, I've heard stories about my feisty grandmother. She loved the color red—evidenced by her choice of hair color. She favored wearing cowboy boots—especially her red pair with the fringe. And she liked nothing better than a rousing game of dominoes.

Yes, the day had blessings, but also regrets. I allowed physical distance and life's circumstances to get in the way of relationship. "Could haves," "should haves," and "if onlys" kept popping into my mind. Could have spent more time. Should have visited more often. If only I had known her better.

One important thing comforts me this evening. As we stood today around the mound of freshly turned up earth, my preacher cousin testified to my grandmother's faith and trust in Jesus. She trusted in Jesus as her Savior and Lord. After living 103 years in time, she now walks with Jesus in eternity, and I will see her again someday.

CLOSING
MATERIALS

Let the Nurturing Begin!

We Conclude Our Study of Lois and Eunice

Let's Pray a Closing Prayer Together

Dear Lord, You are the Master Mentor and Nurturer. Help us always look to You for direction, guidance, and wisdom in mentoring and nurturing faith in our family and loved ones. Teach us to use Your Word to raise and train our grandchildren and children. Use us as Your vessel. Thank You for the precious lives you've entrusted to us to raise to know Your will and Your ways. Often we feel unworthy and inadequate. We know those feelings aren't from You and so we pray for confidence and courage from the Holy Spirit.

Father, please guide us as we seek the next step after this study. Show us how to use what we've learned and put it into practice. We don't want this to be just another study we do and put away on our shelf. We want to mentor and receive mentoring in the way You show us in Your Word. We know that with Your encouragement and direction, anything is possible. Amen.

Janet's Suggestions

Congratulations! You are well on your way to nurturing your family's faith. If you've completed the study "On Your Own," you should feel equipped to mentor or find a mentor. No matter how old your grandchildren, children, or children-of-the-heart, they'll be blessed by your sharing godly wisdom in a loving way.

Also, consider taking another group through this study as the facilitator and leader by utilizing the leader's study guide on page 128. Whatever you do, don't put this study away and forget about it. God had a purpose in leading you to the story of Lois and Eunice. Go back through the book and put on your calendar any commitments you made and make plans to apply points that were especially pertinent to you.

Remember that your grandparenting and parenting is a witness and role model. Always be aware that others are watching to see what a Christian grandparent and parent looks like. Remain alert and open to ways you can serve in ministry.

Use the Prayer & Praise Journal on page 139. Record your spiritual journey and what you have seen the Lord do in your life. For M&M'S, this will be a legacy of your mentoring relationship.

For Further Reading:
- *A Car Seat in My Convertible?* by Sharon Hoffman
- *Generation G* by Marty Norman
- *Missions Moments 2* by Mitzi Eaker
- *Praying for Your Prodigal Daughter: Hope, Help, and Encouragement for Hurting Parents* by Janet Thompson
- *Preparing My Heart for Grandparenting* by Lydia E. Harris
- *The Christian Grandma's Idea Book* by Ellen Banks Elwell
- *The Plan A MOM in a Plan B World* by Debbie Taylor Williams
- *Woman to Woman Mentoring: How to Start, Grow, and Maintain a Mentoring Ministry* DVD Leader Kit by Janet Thompson available at your local LifeWay bookstore or at www.lifeway.com or by calling 1-800-458-2772

Additional "Face-to-Face" Bible studies:
- *Face-to-Face with Mary and Martha: Sisters in Christ*
- *Face-to-Face with Naomi and Ruth: Together for the Journey*
- *Face-to-Face with Elizabeth and Mary: Generation to Generation*
- *Face-to-Face with Euodia and Syntyche: From Conflict to Community*
- *Face-to-Face with Priscilla and Aquila: Balancing Life and Ministry*
- *Face-to-Face with Sarah, Rachel and Hannah: Pleading with God*

To read more of Janet's books:
- *The Team That Jesus Built: How to Develop, Equip, and Commission a Women's Ministry Team*
- *Dear God, Why Can't I Have a Baby? A Companion Guide for Couples on the Infertility Journey*
- *Dear God, They Say It's Cancer: A Companion Guide for Women on the Breast Cancer Journey*

For spiritual gift testing:
- C. Peter Wagner's *Finding Your Spiritual Gifts: Wagner-Modified Houts Questionnaire* (Gospel Light)

To learn more about AHW Ministries, Janet's writing and speaking ministry, visit www.womantowomanmentoring.com and info@womantowomanmentoring.com

LEADER'S GUIDE

for Group-Study
Facilitators and M&M's

Suggestions for Facilitators

Congratulations! God has appointed you the awesome privilege of setting the pace and focus for this group. Regardless of how many groups you have facilitated, this group will be a new and unique experience. This guide's suggestions and tips have helped me, and I trust they also will benefit you. Change or adapt them as you wish, but they are a solid place to start.

Organizing the Sessions

Small groups generally meet in a home, and larger churchwide groups usually meet at the church or other facility. I suggest for the larger group that you form small groups by sitting everyone at round tables. Appoint or ask for a volunteer facilitator for each table and have the group sit together for the five sessions of this study. Then both small-group leaders and large-group table facilitators can use the following format.

1. Starting the sessions—In my experience, members usually come in rushed, harried, and someone is always late—creating the perplexing dilemma of when to start. I suggest beginning on time because you are committed to ending on time. Don't wait for the last late person to arrive. Waiting dishonors those who arrive on time and sets the precedent that it's OK to be a little late because "they won't start without me, anyway." Also, if you delay the start time, you may not finish the discussion.

2. Icebreakers—Each session has an "icebreaker" that is fun, interactive, helps the group become acquainted, and encourages ontime arrivals. It's an interactive activity participants won't want to miss. The icebreaker also eases group members out of their hectic day and into a study mode.

3. Format—Each session includes: Opening Prayer, Icebreaker, Five Days of Selected Discussion Questions, Prayer, Fellowship.

4. The Session Guide provides you with:
- Preparation: what you need to do or obtain in advance.
- Icebreakers: openers for each meeting.
- Bold: the action you need to say or take.
- Ideas: to help facilitate discussion and suggest answers that might be less obvious.
- Session name, day, and page number: to identify area discussed.

5. Suggested time—Each session has nine numbered activities. Fifteen minutes on each number equals a two-hour meeting. This is a guideline to modify according to your time allotment. Let the Holy Spirit guide you and cover what seems applicable and pertinent to your group.

6. Facilitating discussion—Questions and Scriptures to discuss are only a suggestion to enhance what participants have studied on their own already. Feel free to cover whatever material you think or the group feels is pertinent. Think about ways to:
- Keep all engaged in conversation.
- Avoid "rabbit trails."
- Assure each one has a clear understanding of the points under discussion.
- Encourage members to stay accountable by doing their lesson and arriving on time. Big job, you say! You can do it with God's help and strength.

7. Prayertime—Prayer should be an ongoing and vital part of your group. Open and close your times together in prayer. There is a prayer at the end of each session to pray together. Taking prayer requests can often get lengthy and be a source of gossip, if not handled properly. Let me share with you a way that works well in groups:
- At the end of the meeting, give each woman an index card and instruct her to write one prayer request pertaining to the study and pass the card to the leader/facilitator. Mix up the cards and have each person pick one. If someone picks her own card, have her put it back in the pile and pick a different one.
- When everyone has a card, go around the group (or table) and each person is to read the name and prayer request on her card so others can write down the requests. Participants may want to use the Prayer & Praise Journal starting on page 139.
- Instruct the group to hold hands and agree in unison as each participant prays the prayer request for the person whose card she has. This allows everyone to experience praying.
- Each woman takes home the card she received and prays for that person, ongoing.
- As the leader/facilitator, pray between meetings for the group, your leadership, and ask God to mentor you and the members. And have fun!

8. Communion — You will offer communion during the last session (assuming doing so creates no problems in your church context). Remind the group that taking communion together as believers is significant and unifying in three ways, by:
- proclaiming the Lord's death,
- providing an opportunity for fellowship and unity, and
- giving participants an occasion for remembrance of Jesus.

If there are nonbelievers, explain that communion is for believers. This is a perfect opportunity to ask if they would like to accept Jesus Christ as their Savior and pray the Salvation Prayer on page 62. If they are not ready, then ask them to sit quietly while the believers take communion. Ask someone to read aloud the Scriptures in Matthew 26:26–29 or Luke 22:14–20 and have the group partake of the juice and bread at the appropriate spot in the Scripture reading. Matthew 26:30 says, *"When they had sung a hymn they went out to the Mount of Olives."* Close the time of communion with a worship song.

9. Fellowship time — It's important for relationships to develop so group members feel comfortable sharing during discussions. A social time with refreshments provides a nice way to bring closure to the evening and allows time to chat. Encourage everyone to stay. Fellowship is part of the small group experience and allows larger groups to get to know other members.

M & M'S

Use the Session Guide for additional information and help in determining which questions to emphasize during meetings.

SESSION GUIDE

SESSION ONE: THEIR STORY, PAGE 13
- **Go** to http://tinyurl.com/29owaf to obtain lyrics and musical accompaniment for the song "I Know Whom I Have Believed." **Make** copies for each member.
- **Obtain** a whiteboard, markers, and name tags.

1. **Opening Prayer: Hold** hands as a group and **open** in prayer.

2. **Icebreaker: Can You Relate?**
   - **Print** names of women in the Bible onto name tags. **Intermingle** well-known women with some that are lesser known.
   - As group members arrive, **put** a name tag on their back **without telling** them who they have.
   - Members have to ask each other questions about the name and figure out who it is by answers/clues they receive.
   - **Continue** until everyone discovers who is "on her back."

3. **DAY ONE: How Does Lois and Eunice's Story Relate to Us?, Page 15**

Q: **Ask** if anyone has heard of Lois and Eunice before doing this study.

Q: **Discuss** the value in learning about godly grandmothers and mothers and **invite** someone to share how her grandmother or mother influenced her spiritual life.

Q: **Determine** grandmothers, mothers, "community mothers," and spiritual mothers in the group.

4. **DAY TWO: Like Mother, Like Daughter, Page 18**

Q: **Discuss** the ethnic and spiritual heritage of group members and how this influences their faith.

Q: **Read** 1 Corinthians 10:32 and **discuss** the relevance of Paul circumcising Timothy.

Q: **Divide** into a Lois group (grandmothers) and a Eunice group (mothers who aren't yet grandmothers). For those who are neither, **ask** them to be in a group representing Timothy's Greek father. If there is no one for that group, **you take** the role. **Have** the groups act out a speculative dialogue regarding Paul circumcising Timothy.

◆ **Regroup** and **discuss** what group members have willingly given up or sacrificed for the sake of the gospel and how other family members responded.

5. **DAY THREE: Sharing Your Testimony, Page 22**

Q: **Discuss** the differences and similarities in Paul's and Timothy's testimonies. Similarities: both taught Scriptures as children, people knew about and confirmed they were men of faith. Differences: Paul was a Jewish Pharisee persecuting Christians and had a dramatic conversion, while Timothy was raised in a mixed Jewish Christian/Gentile Greek home.

Q: **Ask:** What should be the focus and purpose of testimonies? Answer: God and an opportunity to share the gospel.

Q: **Invite** volunteers to share their speculative testimony for Lois, Eunice, and Timothy.

◆ **Encourage** several to share a personal testimony and who they most resemble.

Q: **Read** Acts 26:25–29; 2 Timothy 1:8–10 and **discuss** how God wants to use each group member's testimony.

◆ **Ask:** What difficulties might you encounter and where will you get the courage?

Q: **Ask:** How do the testimonies of Paul and Timothy encourage that God can use us in spite of faults and/or fears?

Q: **Read** 2 Timothy 1:12. **Stop** and **sing** "I Know Whom I Have Believed."

6. **DAY FOUR: Using Your Gifts for God's Glory, Page 26**

Q: **Discuss** the significance of two churches miles apart telling Paul about Timothy.

Q: **Ask:** How did Timothy become aware of his spiritual gifts?

Q: **Read** 2 Timothy 1:6–7 and 4:2, 5 and **list** Timothy's gifts on a white-board in one column.

♦ In the second column, **list** each member's gifts and how she's using them.

Q: **Ask:** Why does God give us gifts, and what are we to do with them?

Q: **Discuss** who feels she's truly using her gifts for God's glory.

Q: If anyone is unsure of her gifts, **direct** her to page 127 for information on taking a spiritual gifts inventory.

7. DAY FIVE: Mentoring 101, Page 31

Q: **Ask** several group members to describe *mentoring* in their own words.

Q: **Ask** several to share being a mentee of, or mentoring, a family member.

Q: **Ask** someone to read 2 Timothy 1:13 and 2:2 and explain how this is an example of mentoring. Answer: Paul told Timothy to teach what Paul had taught him.

Q: **Go around the room reading** the verses that apply to mentoring and **discuss** answers for how each one applies to Lois, Eunice, Paul, and Timothy.

Q: **Ask:** What is the *only* mentoring or parenting manual needed?
Answer: Bible.

♦ **Discuss** why we sometimes fail to use the Bible as our guide.

Q: **On a whiteboard, title** one column "Mentors" the other "Mentees."
Ask for characteristics of each and list.

♦ After exhausting the list, **ask** who thinks they have characteristics for being a mentor or qualities of a mentee.

Q: **Match** the columns together into M&M relationships for the remainder of this study. Also **ask** them to identify someone in their family to mentor during the study.

8. PRAYERTIME (see Leader's Guide, p. 129).
Prayer requests, prayer partner exchange, and group prayer.

9. FELLOWSHIP AND REFRESHMENTS.

SESSION TWO: NURTURING FAITH IN YOUR FAMILY, PAGE 37

● **Obtain** whiteboard, markers, and note cards.

1. OPENING PRAYER: Hold hands as a group and **open** in prayer.

2. ICEBREAKER:

♦ **Distribute** note cards and **ask** group members to write a fond memory of a grandparent, aunt, or older family member.

♦ **Collect** and **shuffle** the cards. **Distribute, making sure** no one gets her own card.

♦ **Have** each woman read what's on her card and try to guess who wrote it.

3. **DAY ONE: Start Young, Page 38**

Q: **Be sure** everyone understands that as Jews, Lois and Eunice knew the Old Testament Scriptures.

Q: **Discuss** how Lois and Eunice lived out the Scriptures on pages 38-39.

Q: **Ask:** How did Lois and Eunice teaching the Old Testament Scriptures to Timothy prepare them all to accept Christ? Answer: The Old Testament points to Christ.

Q: **Discuss** answering children's spiritual questions.

♦ **Ask** if anyone has a story of a child's spiritual question catching her off guard.

4. **DAY TWO: Lay a Firm Foundation, Page 42**

Q: **Read** Titus 2:3–5. **Make** two columns on a whiteboard and **ask** for examples of the Word of God being maligned today and how following Titus 2:3–5 would make a difference.

Q: **Ask:** How would Lois applying Titus 2:3–5 help Eunice?

Q: **Read** Deuteronomy 6:1–9. On the whiteboard, **number** 1–6 and **ask** for ways to impress the Lord's commandments on children and practical applications for each one.

♦ **Ask** if anyone practices these things in their homes and one they plan to implement.

Q: **Compare** the characteristics of a home built on a righteous foundation with one built on a worldly foundation.

♦ **Discuss** difficulties in barring the world's ways from homes and lives and their solutions.

5. **DAY THREE: Seek Opportunities, Page 47**

Q: **Discuss** prayer and spiritual guidance being more valuable than gifts for children.

Q: **Have** group members read aloud the verses about what Paul gave his "family."

♦ **Discuss** how parents should follow Paul's example.

Q: **Read** 1 Thessalonians 2:11–12. **Write down** on the left side of a whiteboard *E C U* and **have** members complete the words.

♦ **Discuss** opportunities to apply these.

Q: **Stop** and **pray** for all the grandchildren and children represented in the group.

6. **DAY FOUR: Make Learning Fun, Page 50**

Q: **Have** various group members read a psalm and **ask** the reader to give her answer for implementing the message.

Q: **Ask** group members to share and demonstrate how they "make a joyful noise" unto the Lord.

7. **DAY FIVE: Savor Memories, Page 54**

Q: **Be sure** they understand it only takes one generation for something to vanish. **Ask** for examples of "extinct" items from their parent's generation. Examples: transistor radios, vinyl records, cassette tapes, floppy disks, flashbulbs, etc.

◆ **List on a whiteboard** things they think will be outdated in their lifetime. Examples: the post office, newspaper, landlines, etc.

Q: **Discuss** the Ephesian church's rise and fall in three generations and how that can happen in churches today.

Q: **Read** Daniel 4:3. **Ask** what everyone's doing to create and pass down family memories and preserve stories of God's miracles and wonders.

Q: **Discuss** things the group could do to remember their time together in this study.

8. **PRAYERTIME** (see Leader's Guide, p. 129)
    Prayer requests, prayer partner exchange, and group prayer.

9. **FELLOWSHIP AND REFRESHMENTS**

SESSION THREE: MODELING FAITH FOR YOUR FAMILY, PAGE 59

● **Obtain** whiteboard, markers.
● **Use** http://www.kididdles.com/lyrics/t030.html for words and music to the song "This Little Light of Mine." **Make** copies of lyrics for group members.
● **Provide** a candle for each team member, and a lighter.

1. **OPENING PRAYER: Hold** hands as a group and **open** in prayer.

2. **ICEBREAKER:**
◆ **Turn off** lights and **light** one single candle.
◆ **Ask:** In the dark, where does your focus go? As they answer, "The candle," **point out** that's how Christians appear in a dark world.
◆ **Set** a lit candle in front of each woman; let it shine during today's meeting.
◆ **Turn on** the lights.

3. **DAY ONE: Family Ties, Page 60**

Q: **Determine** if there are "spiritually single" women in your group and **ask** what comfort they derive from Eunice.

◆ If theirs was not a similar experience, **ask** how the group can support and pray for them.

Q: **Ask** various women to summarize the faith journeys of the biblical families on pages 60-61, **emphasizing** the risk and the rewards, especially for Rahab.

Q: **Read** Proverbs 18:24. **Discuss** what it means to be brothers and sisters in Christ in the church, the family, and this group.

♦ If someone isn't a believer, **ask** if she would like to pray the Salvation Prayer now, or if she did already. **Celebrate** and **welcome** her into the family of God.

4. **DAY TWO: As for Me and My House . . . Page 64**

Q: **Discuss** Paul's directives on households.

Q: **Do** a group reading of Joshua 24:1–31 and **compare** the difficulty of permanently renouncing idols and detestable practices for the Israelites and us today.

♦ **List** on the whiteboard the group's examples of each.

♦ **Ask** if anyone has unsuccessfully tried renouncing one of these and needs accountability. **Try to get** everyone to pick one item.

♦ **Stop** and **pray**, **asking** the Holy Spirit to provide strength and courage to permanently eliminate these idols and practices. Then **cross a line through** each one mentioned, signifying overcoming.

♦ **Talk about** ways to adapt this concept in their homes.

Q: **Invite** each member to share one family tradition passed down through the generations. For those who can't think of one, what tradition could they start? **Suggest** a Sunday supper.

5. **DAY THREE: Let Your Light Shine, Page 69**

Q: **Ask** three members to **read** Isaiah 58:10; Matthew 5:15–17; and 2 Corinthians 4:5–7. **Discuss** the meaning of "let your light shine."

Q: **Read** Ruth 1:1–18. **Discuss** the questions pertaining to this passage.

Q: **Ask:** Whose light was shown into Timothy's life, and what was he to do with his own light?

Q: **Have** each woman hold up the candle in front of her as everyone **sings**, "This Little Light of Mine."

6. **DAY FOUR: Daughters- and Sons-of-the-Heart, Page 72**

Q: **Ask:** What terms does John use to describe believers? Answer: Children, friends, brothers.

Q: **Ask:** What did Naomi call Ruth and Paul call Timothy?

Q: **Discuss** what it means to be in the family of God.

Q: **Discuss** scenarios where someone would be a "community" mother. Examples: Girl Scouts, Young Life, small groups.

♦ **Ask** if anyone has been in this role, or a spiritual mother-of-the-heart, and the results.

7. **DAY FIVE: Follow My Example, Page 76**

Q: **Read** Pastor Brian Smith's opening quote and **discuss** the application to grandparents and parents.

Q: **Ask:** How was Timothy to follow Paul?

♦ **Ask:** Was Paul arrogant telling his followers to follow him? Who was Paul following?

Q: **Read** Hebrews 13:7. **Ask:** Whose life are you imitating?

Q: **Have** each woman **read** the statement and **fill in** her name: Follow my
_____'s example as I _____ follow the example of Christ.

♦ **Discuss** how it felt saying this and who's following each woman's example.

♦ **Reinforce** that followers of Jesus lead others to follow Him.

Q: **Conclude** by **discussing** the encouragement of knowing that we don't
have to be perfect, but we do need to live a life that glorifies God.

♦ **Write on the whiteboard** the words *speech*, *life*, *love*, *faith*, and *purity* and
ask each woman to state one area she's improving because her grandchildren, children, and the family of God are watching.

8. **PRAYERTIME** (see Leader's Guide, p. 129)
Prayer requests, prayer partner exchange, and group prayer.

9. **FELLOWSHIP AND REFRESHMENTS**

SESSION FOUR: PARENTING PRODIGALS, PAGE 83

● **Obtain** whiteboard and markers.

1. **OPENING PRAYER: Hold** hands as a group and **open** in prayer.

2. **ICEBREAKER:**
Q: **Go** through alphabet, **having** each woman state an attribute of God that
starts with the next letter and continue for all the letters. For example:
A—awesome, B—benevolent.

3. **DAY ONE: We Did the Best We Could, Page 84**
Q: **Ask** if anyone is dealing with a prodigal and **be sensitive** to her during
today's discussion.

Q: **Read 2 Timothy 2:22. On the whiteboard, label** one column "Evil Desire"
the other "Righteous Desire." **Ask** for their lists in each column and **discuss** ways to encourage children to develop healthy desires.

Q: **Discuss** the spiritual lives of biblical parents with prodigals and how,
even with godly parents, children make mistakes.

Q: **Ask** what changes each woman wants to make in her parenting.

♦ **Point out** that if there aren't prodigals in the group, this session contains
biblical parenting and preventative tips.

4. **DAY TWO: Pray Daily and Persistently, Page 88**
Q: **Practice** personalizing prayer using the Scriptures on page 88-89, and
have each woman insert the name of her grandchild or child.

Q: **Stop** and **pray** for any women struggling with prodigals.

5. **DAY THREE: Love Unconditionally, Page 91**
Q: **Write** on the whiteboard and **discuss** answers for the "Elements of
Love" and ways to "Display to a Prodigal."

Q: **Talk about** God showing unconditional love when we were prodigals
before accepting Christ or after.

Q: **Break into pairs** and **have** each pair take turns admonishing and encouraging in love.

♦ **Regroup** and **discuss** which was the easiest and most natural.

6. **DAY FOUR: Practice Forgiveness, Page 94**

Q: **Ask:** How are you at forgiving or do you hold a grudge?

Q: **Have** each woman **read** a verse on forgiveness and **discuss** how it applies to Lois and Eunice and to her own life.

Q: **Ask:** How does it feel when someone forgives you? When God forgives you?

7. **DAY FIVE: Don't Give Up!, Page 97**

Q: **Have** someone **read** Malachi 4:5–6 and **discuss** the message.

Q: **Read** Proverbs 1:1–7 and **write** numbers 1–6 on the whiteboard. **Ask** for ways Proverbs could help them be a better grandparent, parent, or community parent.

Q: **Take turns reading** the verses on page 98. **Discuss** their message of hope.

Q: **Ask** the group to commit to reading a chapter in Proverbs daily for a month and apply to parenting.

8. **PRAYERTIME** (see Leader's Guide, p. 129).
Prayer requests, prayer partner exchange, and group prayer.

9. **FELLOWSHIP AND REFRESHMENTS.**

SESSION FIVE: RAISING UP THE NEXT GENERATION IN THE CHURCH FAMILY, PAGE 101

● **Obtain** whiteboard and markers.

1. **OPENING PRAYER: Hold** hands as a group and **open** in prayer.

2. **ICEBREAKER:**

♦ **Ask** for testimonies of reading a chapter in Proverbs daily.

3. **DAY ONE: Recognizing Young Leaders, Page 102**

Q: **Ask:** Why didn't Paul take John Mark with him, and why was Paul so impressed with Timothy?

♦ If they're not sure of the answer, **read** the verses on what was important to Paul in a potential leader and worker for Christ. Answer: perseverance and willingness to suffer, endure hardships, and stick it out.

Q: **Suggest** that sometimes trainees can disappoint. **Ask** for alternatives to giving up on them.

Q: **Ask** for testimonies of someone seeing potential and encouraging them when they were young.

4. DAY TWO: Developing an Apprentice, Page 106

Q: **Discuss** the value of having an apprentice.

♦ **Have** different women paraphrase Ecclesiastes 4:8–10 and **apply** to: work, ministry, parenting, marriage, friendships, and teams.

5. DAY THREE: **Training, Equipping, Commissioning, Page 110**

Q: **Label** two columns on the whiteboard: "Area of Ministry" and "Upbringing." **Have** them fill in each column for the Scripture passages listed.

Q: **Have fun** seeing which Be-attitude they matched with a Scripture. **Look up** and **clarify** any discrepancies.

Q: **Ask** several to share how they're preparing children for going out on their own. **Ask** others how, or if, they were prepared by their parents.

6. DAY FOUR: **Passing the Torch and Baton, Page 114**

Q: **Discuss** the emotions Lois and Eunice felt knowing Timothy could be in danger.

♦ **Ask** how they would feel about their own children taking such a risk for the Lord.

Q: **Review** the points in Paul's final charge to Timothy in 2 Timothy 4:1–2, 5.

Q: **Ask** for testimonies of a Paul/Timothy and a Lois/Eunice relationship. Does anyone feel she has this with her grandchild or child?

7. DAY FIVE: **Mentoring Is Not an Option, Page 119**

Q: **Ask:** After doing this study, do you agree that mentoring isn't an option, especially in families? **Discuss** answers.

Q: **Discuss** group member's experiences in the mentoring relationships established in session one, and any family mentoring relationship that developed.

Q: **Read** Deuteronomy 4:9–10 and Psalm 71:17–18 and **discuss** answers to the questions pertaining to these verses.

Q: **Ask** what they have seen God do in their life during this study and in their mentoring relationships. **Make** a "Thanks for the Memories" list on the whiteboard and **have** someone copy it for everyone.

♦ **Plan** a closing potluck inviting everyone's families. **Have** each member bring a favorite "traditional" food from her family and one item passed down through the generations. After dinner, **ask** each woman to share what she put on the "Thanks for the Memories" list.

8. PRAYERTIME (see Leader's Guide, p. 129)

♦ **Take** Communion together (see p. 130).

♦ **Read** the closing prayer on page 126 together.

9. FELLOWSHIP AND REFRESHMENTS.

♦ **Talk** about the study the group wants to do next. **See** page 127 for additional "Face-to-Face" Bible studies.

Prayer & Praise Journal

Prayer & Praise Journal

Prayer & Praise Journal

Prayer & Praise Journal

New Hope® Publishers is a division of WMU®, an international organization that challenges Christian believers to understand and be radically involved in God's mission. For more information about WMU, go to www.wmu.com. More information about New Hope books may be found at www.newhopedigital.com. New Hope books may be purchased at your local bookstore.

If you've been blessed by this book, we would like to hear your story. The publisher and author welcome your comments and suggestions at: newhopereader@wmu.org

Other New Hope Bible Studies for Women

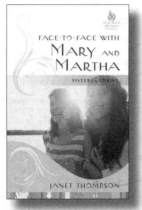

Face-to-Face with Mary and Martha
Sisters in Christ
Janet Thompson
ISBN-10: 1-59669-254-5
ISBN-13: 978-1-59669-254-1

Chosen and Cherished
Becoming the Bride of Christ
*Edna Ellison, Joy Brown,
and Kimberly Sowell*
ISBN-10: 1-59669-271-5
ISBN-13: 978-1-59669-271-8

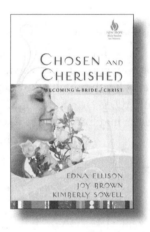

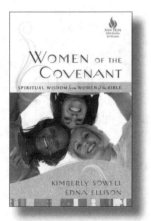

Women of the Covenant
Spiritual Wisdom from Women of the Bible
Kimberly Sowell and Edna Ellison
ISBN-10: 1-59669-270-7
ISBN-13: 978-1-59669-270-1

Available in bookstores everywhere

For information about these books or any New Hope product,
visit www.newhopedigital.com.